Decorative Woodcarving

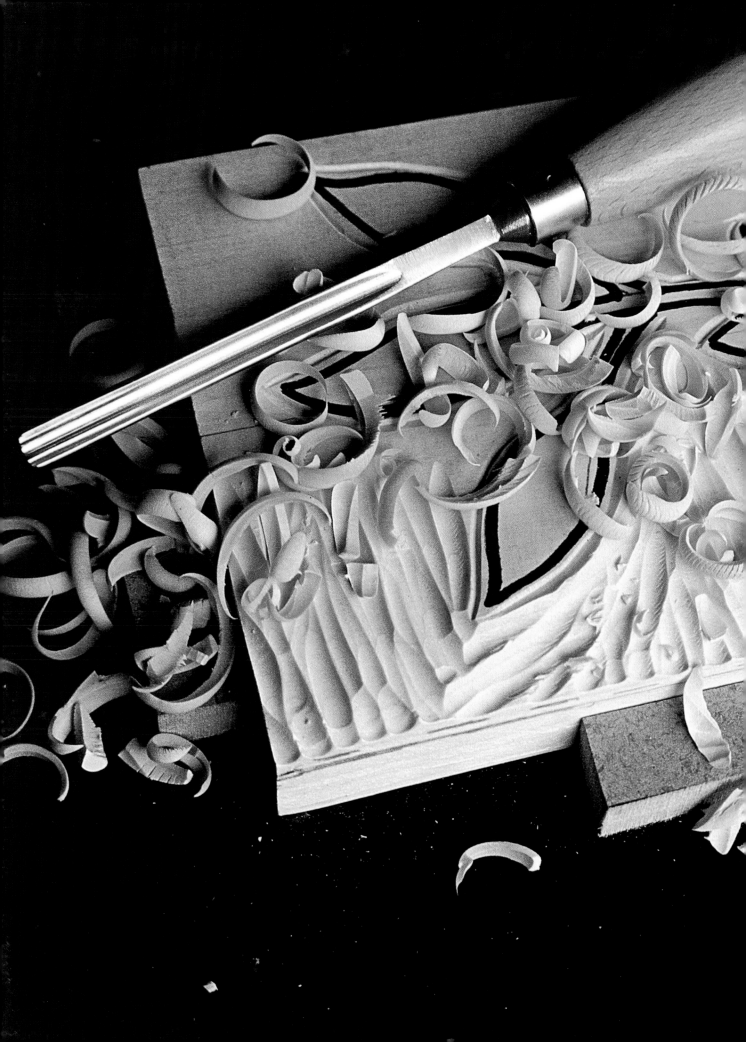

New Edition

Decorative Woodcarving

Jeremy Williams

GUILD OF MASTER CRAFTSMAN PUBLICATIONS LTD

This edition published 2002 by
Guild of Master Craftsman Publications Ltd
Castle Place, 166 High Street,
Lewes, East Sussex BN7 1XU

First edition published 1994
Reprinted 1995, 1999, 2001

ISBN 1 86108 293 2
(First edition ISBN 0 946819 47 5)

Edited by Stephen Haynes
Book and cover designed by Ian Hunt Design
Cover photography by Anthony Bailey
Set in Helvetica

Colour origination by Viscan Graphics (Singapore)
Printed and bound by Kyodo Printing (Singapore)

dedication

This book is dedicated to those wonderful things called trees.

Through the skill of our craftsmanship and the beauty of our work may the Spirit of the Tree live on.

acknowledgements

My thanks are due to a number of companies who assisted me during the course of writing this book, including:

● Ashley Iles (Edge Tools) Ltd for permission to reproduce their photographs

● Henry Taylor (Tools) Ltd for permission to reproduce their carving-tool chart and for supplying samples for photography

● Craft Supplies Ltd for permission to reproduce their chart of Swiss carving tools

● Kurt Koch, Eulenbis, Germany, for details of the Koch sharpening system

● Liberon Waxes Ltd for permission to reproduce text from their catalogue and for kindly verifying my data on wood dyes.

I am indebted to William Sampson, the editor of *Fine Woodworking* magazine, and American carver Fred Cogelow for providing details of American woods. Likewise, I thank Tom Darby of Wamberal, New South Wales for the information on Australian carving woods.

My thanks to all the carvers who kindly gave permission to reproduce photographs of their work.

Thanks to art historian Rozanne Arnold for checking historical facts, and to William Chapman for dealing with aspects of technical drawing.

I am grateful to my friend Mike Fairclough for his help with photography, and to my editor, Stephen Haynes of GMC Publications.

To my wife, Jeane, my special thanks for her unstinting support.

Finally, my thanks to all the other individuals and companies who assisted me in producing this book.

contents

safe woodcarving

When performed correctly, woodcarving is a relatively safe activity. But it is naturally wise to take a few simple precautions, especially when you are using power tools.

You should therefore observe the following safety points *at all times*:

● **Always hold chisels and gouges correctly,** so that your fingers are *behind* the cutting edge of the blade. Never hold your tools or work with your hands in front of the blade.

● **Always cut away from yourself.** Never reverse a carving tool and cut towards your body, no matter how tempting this may seem. It is far safer to turn the wood round to a new position.

● **Keep your tools razor-sharp.** Not only will they require less energy to drive them through the wood, but there is less chance of their skating over the surface. Blunt tools can easily slip and slide dangerously. What is more, if you are unlucky enough to cut yourself, the wound from a sharp blade heals more quickly than that made by a blunt blade.

● **Don't work in a clutter.** Give yourself room to move, and only have a few tools out on the bench at any time.

● **Secure your carving wood firmly** before you start to work.

● **Sweep up** after every session. It is uncomfortable to stand on wood chips for too long, and you may slip.

● **Throw away rags** used for applying oil or wax immediately after use. They can be highly combustible.

Dirty wire wool can reputedly self-ignite, so don't keep old bits.

● **Adequate lighting and ventilation** are important – make sure your workplace has both.

● **Never carve when you are tired** or when your concentration is at a low ebb.

● **Safety glasses** approved for high impact should be worn, especially when working with power tools. If you normally wear spectacles, buy a pair of ventilated safety goggles.

● **Use a dust mask** approved for hardwood fibres. Wood dust, even in small quantities, can irritate your eyes and nose. Prolonged exposure can have a lasting detrimental effect.

● **Wear approved ear muffs** when using power tools, as the noise can be harmful.

● **Get into the habit of using these safety aids** when bandsawing, routing, drilling, sanding or grinding, even if only for a few minutes.

● **Keep solvents in clearly marked containers**, well out of reach of small children.

● **Lock up** your workshop when it is not in use.

● **Don't rush.** A good craftsmen never hurries.

● **An approved fire extinguisher** for use with electrical appliances is a wise investment.

● **A first-aid kit is a must.** Remember to replace items as soon as they are used.

introduction

Go into the old churches and stately homes of England, or the cathedrals of France, Spain or Germany, and you will find many fine examples of decorative carving. Or perhaps look at the beautiful work produced by craftsmen in India, China or Japan; by the Maori carvers of New Zealand; or the work from Bali and Polynesia. Even in today's busy world there are still many quiet corners where men and women use the traditional methods of relief carving to express their artistic ideas.

Unfortunately, though, many carvers, and particularly beginners, tend to overlook the techniques which can be generalized as 'decorative woodcarving', and in doing so deny themselves much scope for expressing their ideas. Wood is not as malleable as clay, and doesn't have the inherent strength of bronze, so it is sometimes impossible to produce an idea in a three-dimensional form satisfactorily by carving in the round. But by working in relief virtually all designs are possible. The techniques described in this book are traditional, and can be used for a wide array of ornamental and functional purposes: panels and wall plaques, screens, furniture decoration, and even everyday items like breadboards.

Many books have been written about wood sculpture, but in recent years there seem to have been few devoted solely to decorative forms of carving. This seems to me a very great pity, for there is no doubt that by learning the techniques commonly used by carvers in days gone by, one's carving skill can be greatly improved. There is also the added bonus that these techniques can be useful when texture treatments have to be applied to three-dimensional work.

Decorative carving is an extensive subject, and many volumes could be filled with practical examples, but when the basic techniques are examined and analysed they divide into clear and simple categories: low relief, high relief, incised, intaglio, and pierced carving. And one of the virtues is that none of the various techniques is difficult to learn.

● **Low relief** is undoubtedly the most popular style, and is widely used in furniture carving. Basically it consists of removing a minimal amount of background wood – usually not more than ¼in (6mm) at most – to create the contours of the chosen pattern.

● **High-relief carving**, as the term implies, requires the removal of a greater depth of background – usually around 1–2in (25–50mm), but at times the working depth needed may be more. In extreme cases a high-relief carving can assume virtually three-dimensional proportions, and be built up with blocks glued to the background wood.

● **Incised carving** in its simplest form is literally drawing a design with a cutting tool on the surface of the wood. This technique is useful when a totally flat surface must be retained, such as a chair seat or back, or for a simple picture. However, incised carving can be more effective if some contour modelling is carried out in the actual design – a treatment known as *modified incised carving*. Another method of decorating a flat surface is to use chip-carving techniques, which employ geometric designs made with angular incised cuts.

● **Intaglio work** involves producing a negative image, and is mainly used for creating designs on items such as butter moulds. The treatment can also be effective for areas of detail, such as small leaves, incorporated in a relief carving.

● **Pierced carving** is the technique employed when wood not forming part of the actual design is removed by a series of cut-outs. It is similar to fretwork, and can be used for screens or wall plaques.

Over the many years I have instructed beginners, my approach has been to introduce the basic guidelines of technique, and then encourage the student to interpret his or her own design. Why be obliged to carve an oak leaf, just because I say so, when you really want to carve a rose? In this book I have adopted the same method.

There are practical instructions for each technique, but it is up to you, the reader, to formulate your own design or reproduce the example used, as you choose. Whichever course you take, I very much hope you will enjoy the experience. This is not intended to be a book of designs and patterns, but rather the means to help you embark on a voyage of adventure into decorative carving. My objective is to allow the reader (whether an accomplished craftsman in other forms of woodwork, or a complete beginner) to learn something of lasting value about this art form.

For the benefit of readers new to carving, this book not only covers the actual techniques, but also ranges over the selection of suitable woods, and the choice of tools and their care. These are fundamental to success. Both styling and technical drawing are covered, as well as suitable finishing treatments, including the use of colour.

On page viii you will find advice on safety. Carving should not be a dangerous activity, but it obviously pays to take care when you are using sharp tools and mechanical cutting instruments. **Please read this section carefully before you attempt any carving.**

Finally, a note on how the dimensions used in this book are described. Since it is not written for any specific group, there will clearly be some readers who prefer to work in inches and others who use metric measurements. I have chosen to indicate both, but for obvious purposes I have on occasion opted to use the nearest practical metric equivalent rather than a true conversion.

introduction to the new edition

This new edition has allowed the use of full-colour pictures, which will help the reader new to carving to progress speedily in a new-found craft.

It has also given me the opportunity to revise some parts of the book to take into account both new products and changes in technique that have become popular since the first edition was produced.

I have expanded the treatment of low-relief carving in Chapter 8 with a second project. This allows readers new to carving to gain confidence through working on a design more complex than the first low-relief project, but one which is still relatively straightforward in its construction.

For the same reason there is more information now about carving flat surfaces, which will, I trust, be of use to hobby furniture-makers who may wish to embellish the product of their labour.

On the subject of dimensions and measurements, we still have both metric and imperial widely in use, so I have chosen to leave this matter unaltered from the first edition. Those readers who are used to only one form of calibration will, I hope, bear with me.

Lastly, may I wish you, the reader, every success. The carving of wood can be and should be highly satisfying, but it will at times be challenging as well. If it was not, it would not be such fun!

Jeremy Williams
CORNWALL, ENGLAND 2002

part one
getting
started

"The more you get to know your woods,

the better your carvings will be."

1 historical aspects

The decision to take up woodcarving is usually combined with a great enthusiasm to seize a piece of wood and just get going. This is fine if you simply want to whittle away, but for anything more adventurous you will undoubtedly find it useful to look at the history of carving and the types of work done through the ages. Even a brief study will help you to answer vital questions such as 'What shall I carve?' and 'In what style shall I carve it?' and give you an understanding of why certain tools or species of wood are more suitable for one style of work than another. It is also inspiring, as you admire a beautiful old carving, to think that it was created by somebody who was also once a complete beginner!

Nobody knows precisely when wood was first carved, but it is reasonable to assume that it was practised by primitive man – if only to notch his club every time he battered a sabre-toothed tiger. As wood is a perishable material, however, any examples of prehistoric woodcarving have long since vanished. You can still see examples of Egyptian tomb carvings dating back more than 4,000 years, but these are not really decorative woodcarvings in the modern sense of the phrase.

The real history of decorative carving starts in the early medieval era, with the Saxons and Normans. Quality of workmanship has always been governed by the availability of suitable tools, and it is interesting to note that carvings from the tenth and eleventh centuries differ very much in execution from those of later periods, purely because early work was carried out by carpenters using only simple chisels.

By the thirteenth and fourteenth centuries purpose-made carving tools had been developed, and with them an increasing mastery of carving techniques. At this point carving styles began to diversify as craftsmen became influenced by different architectural styles, but two main themes emerged: the Gothic and the classical. The popularity of these two rival schools has waxed and waned down the centuries, following the dictates of fashion, and at times they have even been intermingled, with somewhat dubious results.

The Gothic style can be traced to north European influences, which were spread far and wide by the warlike races of the region. For centuries past,

Vikings, Danes and other marauders had rampaged around with considerable enthusiasm, carrying with them the aesthetic ideals of their culture. For example, in AD 911 one Rurik the Jute led an excursion into Russia and founded a dynasty that reigned for some 600 years, taking with him northern ideas of decoration to combine with the eastern styles of the conquered territory.

Though early Gothic carving, such as may be seen in many late Norman churches, was executed in a somewhat heavy manner, this school developed to produce open tracery work of fine quality. By the time of the early Tudors in the late fifteenth century, the Perpendicular Gothic style was extensively used in architectural carving. Craftsmen used woods which were readily available locally, such as oak, ash and elm.

Another milestone of the fifteenth century was the interest in trying to reproduce the look of fabric in wood. This led to the development of the well-known linenfold pattern (Fig 1.1), which was extensively used both for architectural panelling and for decorative embellishment on furniture.

One of the greatest exponents of the Gothic style of carving (indeed, one of the two greatest carvers ever known) was Tilman Riemenschneider. Born in southern

Germany in 1460, Riemenschneider devoted most of his adult life to the creation of extraordinarily detailed religious carvings (Fig 1.2). Up until his death in 1531 he worked consistently in the area lying between Salzburg, Munich and Frankfurt, where many of his carvings can still be seen in churches.

Meanwhile, in the eastern Mediterranean, the classical style of carving was becoming standard. Derived from the classical art of early Roman times, it acquired strong classical Greek and even Persian influences after the Roman emperor Constantine transferred his seat of government to Byzantium (now Istanbul) in AD 324. The Greek acanthus-leaf motif (Fig 1.3) became the bedrock of decorative carving in this region for the next thousand years, used either on its own or linked with Christian symbols.

By the middle of the sixteenth century, carvers in western Europe were beginning to turn their backs on the schematic thought of medieval Gothic styles and were looking to the classical style for inspiration. The new influence began in Italy and rapidly spread to neighbouring countries, gaining a particularly strong foothold in the Low Countries. The transition did not happen overnight, though, and for some time the pendulum swung to and

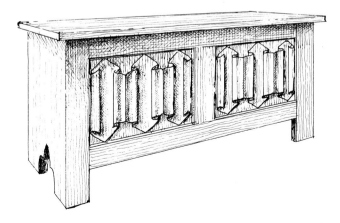 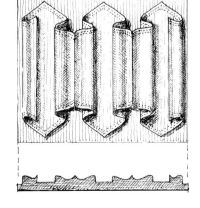

Fig 1.1 *In the fifteenth century linenfold carving was very popular as an embellishment for panelling and furniture*

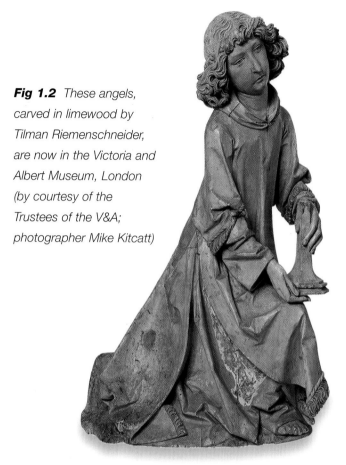

Fig 1.2 *These angels, carved in limewood by Tilman Riemenschneider, are now in the Victoria and Albert Museum, London (by courtesy of the Trustees of the V&A; photographer Mike Kitcatt)*

fro between the Italian/Flemish classical style and Gothic patterns. Spain played an important role in the spread of the new ideas. It was a dominant force in European politics during this period, and many Flemish craftsmen went to work on Spanish churches and cathedrals.

In England, classically inspired styles really became popular following the restoration of the monarchy in 1660. Charles II brought European ideas with him from his exile in France; his successor, William III (William and Mary), imported Dutch tastes from his home in the

Fig 1.3 *The acanthus leaf is still a familiar motif in woodcarving*

Netherlands. After the strictures of the Puritans, a new decorative style was received with considerable relief and pleasure, and Italian curvilinear designs were much in demand. Cabinetmakers emerged as craftsmen in their own right, whereas previously most furniture had been made by joiners.

The seventeenth-century expansion of commercial frontiers was also important, not least because woods other than common native species became more readily available. Although oak continued to be favoured for architectural work, limewood (linden) and pearwood were increasingly used for decorative carving in the latter part of the century. By the early 1700s walnut had become popular, imported from both mainland Europe and North America. Mahogany was also beginning to be used.

The period from around 1730 to the early 1800s is truly described as the golden age of woodcarving. Carvers were elevated beyond the ranks of joiners, and even cabinetmakers. They were able to dictate how things should be carved, rather than working to prescribed

Fig 1.4 *Grinling Gibbons's famous limewood carving of a lace cravat dates from around 1690 (by courtesy of the Trustees of the V&A)*

designs. Gilding was held in high regard, so carvers either worked closely with gilders or did the gilding themselves. The rich and noble spent money on decorative carving at a phenomenal rate, as much to indicate their status as for any appreciation of the craftsmanship involved.

English carving of this period was much enriched by the work of Grinling Gibbons, who, jointly with Riemenschneider, can lay claim to the title of 'the world's best carver' (Fig 1.4). Born in Rotterdam in 1648 of English parents, Gibbons moved to England at the age of 20 and worked there until his death in 1721. Here he established a unique style of carving which, while classical in foundation, eschewed the symmetrical and well-tested

proportions of the true classical style in favour of exuberant asymmetry. High-relief swags embellished with swirls and curls are typical of the work. He used flowers of every type with total abandon, and even carved nutmegs and other fruits. Cherubs bound forth through clusters of fruits, and birds peck at seed heads with natural grace.

This flamboyancy burst upon conservative architects and patrons like a thunderclap, shaking them from their resistance to change. Gibbons was an avid collector of paintings, so contemporary artists may well have inspired him, but he was undoubtedly indebted to the architect Sir Christopher Wren (1632–1723) for his rise to prominence, and other support came from the diarist

Fig 1.5 *An extravagantly carved chair, typical of the Chippendale style (by courtesy of the Trustees of the V&A)*

John Evelyn. With friends of such eminence, Gibbons soon gained royal patronage.

Much of Gibbons's work was carried out in the opulent, dramatic and exciting baroque style, but he was also capable of more restrained carving. His prodigious output led to the belief that he employed many carvers rather than undertaking all the work himself, and this theory was recently reinforced when restoration work was carried out after a fire at Hampton Court Palace near London. On taking down some fire-damaged carvings, it was discovered that some of the pieces had originally

been fixed together upside down – surely the work of an apprentice rather than a master craftsman.

The rococo period which followed the baroque was in some ways more restrained in style, with spirals and diagonal elements depicted less strongly. It was particularly popular in France, but Thomas Johnson, who died around 1778, was a well-known carver of English rococo work.

During this golden age of carving the art of cabinetmaking also came to the fore. Men like Thomas Chippendale (1718–89) and his son, also Thomas

Fig 1.6 The carving of Hepplewhite furniture is more restrained (by courtesy of the Trustees of the V&A)

(1749–1822), used decorative carving extravagantly on their furniture (Fig 1.5). George Hepplewhite, who died in 1786, was also fond of carving on furniture, but used it in a more restrained manner (Fig 1.6). Duncan Phyfe (1768–1854) is regarded by many as the greatest of all American cabinetmakers. Much of his work is decorated with carved leaves, lions' feet, dogs' feet, Prince of Wales feathers, wheat ears, and other embellishments.

But carvers were by no means limited to architectural work and furniture decoration. During the Georgian period one's means of transportation became a way of keeping up with fashion, so carriages, cabs and sedan chairs were all emblazoned with every known device and intricate carving – the Coronation Coach is a familiar example.

During Queen Victoria's reign (1837–1901) the Industrial Revolution saw the introduction of more advanced production methods. Machines now handled much of the hard and repetitive work. A carving machine patented in England in 1845 is thought to have been developed to cope with the enormous volume of repetitive carving entailed in the restoration of the Houses of Parliament; another was patented in America in 1848.

Victorian carving primarily followed the nostalgic fashion of copying 'antique' styles redolent of the 'glorious past', and much of this imitation was not carried out with spectacular expertise. There was a Gothic revival (correctly known as 'Gothick' to distinguish it from the real thing), and a fondness for over-embellishment which does not always appeal to modern tastes (Fig 1.7). The Victorian love of dead game birds and other victims of the chase may seem equally unappealing, but nevertheless useful ideas for subjects can be found by studying nineteenth-century carvings. At the other end of the scale, William Morris (1834–96) did much to initiate a handcraft revival through the Arts and Crafts movement during this period. One of the effects of this was to restore respect for furniture of simple design.

After the First World War fashion swung away from decorative carving, and its intensive labour element had in any case become too costly. More functional styles evolved in the mid-1920s, followed by the Utility furniture of the 1940s and 1950s. The Scandinavian furniture popular in the 1960s was equally unsuited to decorative carving, so for much of the twentieth century the craft experienced bleak years of decline.

But to some degree the wheel of fortune is turning once more. Decorative carving is creeping back, little by little, and is beginning to be seen on furniture in modest amounts. The future looks brighter now than for many years. And in the mean time, we are fortunate in having a wealth of carving history to study in our churches, public buildings, museums, stately homes, and even antique shops. Looking at the work of past craftsmen, both well known and anonymous, stimulates ideas and extends the horizons of carvers today.

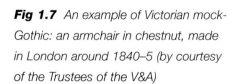

Fig 1.7 *An example of Victorian mock-Gothic: an armchair in chestnut, made in London around 1840–5 (by courtesy of the Trustees of the V&A)*

2 choosing the right wood

While in theory it is possible to carve all and every species of wood, clearly some are more suitable than others. Knowing something about the structure of timber, and about how trees grow, will pay dividends when you actually start carving. Also, it is important to know how to choose the right wood for the work you plan to do, and how to store it so it stays in prime condition.

In the timber trade the broad-leaved types are categorized as **hardwoods** and those with needle-shaped leaves as **softwoods**. But it is important to remember these are only general descriptions – they may have little bearing on whether the wood is either hard or soft. For example, lime, or its American cousin basswood, is one of the easiest woods to carve, yet because it is a broad-leaved tree it comes into the hardwood listing. Yew, on the other hand, being a needle-leaved evergreen, is categorized as a softwood, although it is a hard wood indeed to work with cutting tools.

Many timber suppliers include details of the wood's density in their catalogues, usually shown as a figure of specific gravity or an indication of weight per cubic foot or metre. For precise identification, the Latin botanical name of the wood is also included. Lime and oak, for example, would be listed as:

● **Lime** (*Tilia* spp), 34lb/ft³, 540kg/m³, SG 0.54
● **Oak** (*Quercus* spp), 45lb/ft³, 720kg/m³, SG 0.67

This clearly shows that lime is less dense than oak.

But, while it can be useful to know the density figures if, say, you want to carve a rare wood for the first time, it is simpler to select a wood if you know its carving quality – easy to work, moderately hard, or hard – and whether or not it is capable of accepting fine detail (see the list on pages 22–4).

Timber can be broadly divided into three main groups, relating to where and how the trees originally grew. The warmer and moister the climate, the more quickly a tree will grow, which affects the type of wood to be obtained from it.

● **Temperate climate** Trees from temperate climate zones, such as Europe and parts of North America, can be either broad-leaved deciduous varieties, which drop their leaves in winter, or members of the conifer family, with needle-shaped leaves, which commonly are evergreen. Most of the popular carving woods are broad-leaved species.

● **Equatorial climate** Tropical trees are those which come from all the equatorial zones of the world. Generally they are known as **tropical hardwoods**. They range from varieties producing rare and exotic woods, such as rosewood, through to the more well-known mahogany types. Though widely used in the past, many are now listed as endangered species – although some timber suppliers conform to a policy of only buying from areas of reafforestation.

● **Cold climate** These are the trees which come either from the colder zones of the world, such as Scandinavia, the Baltic countries and Canada, or which grow in a temperate climate but at a high altitude. Though they may not be used extensively for carving in Britain, in their home countries they are popular. Generally they fall into the softwood classification.

How wood is formed

In simple terms, all trees, irrespective of where they grow, have similar component parts (Fig 2.1). There is an outer protective casing, the **bark**; a growing area, **sapwood**; and an inert stable section for upright strength, **heartwood**. Many trees also have a central **core** or **pith**. Of these, the only part which is of any real value for carving is the heartwood. The prime part typically lies about 2in (50mm) in from both the sapwood and the central core (Fig 2.2).

All wood is made up of cells, used by trees for holding nutriment in solution and for water storage. Generally they are similar to bundles of drinking straws. It is important for the carver to know how well the cells are bonded together, since this affects the quality of work that can be produced (see page 21).

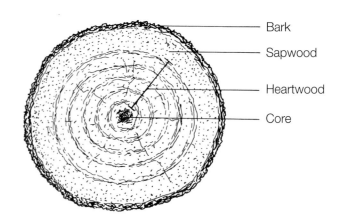

Fig 2.1 *Horizontal cross section of tree trunk showing main component parts*

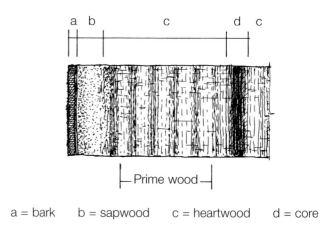

a = bark   b = sapwood   c = heartwood   d = core

Fig 2.2 *Vertical cross section of tree trunk showing prime heartwood area*

While most cells run vertically through the trunk, they also follow the way the branches grow. Some trees have pronounced storage cells which lie more horizontally. These are **medullary rays**, which can be decorative in furniture, but to the carver are more a source of trouble than an advantage. Their density is quite different from the surrounding wood, and they are invariably lines of weakness.

Annual rings

Every year throughout its life a tree grows, increasing not only in height but also in the girth of its trunk. The amount of growth is dependent upon external factors, such as the amount of rainfall, ambient temperature, and the number of hours of sunlight. This cycle of growth can be seen as annual rings when a tree is felled.

There are two periods in the year when trees living in temperate climates actually grow, and the pronounced climatic variation between winter and summer affects the growth cycle. Most new wood is formed in spring and early summer – **spring growth** – but later in the year secondary growth takes place, forming **late wood**. The annual rings reflect this growth pattern: spring growth is represented by wider bands, as this is when the bulk of new wood is formed, while narrower bands show late growth (Fig 2.3).

You should note that late-growth bands tend to be darker, because the wood contains more resin and is harder than spring growth. The difference is most marked in conifers, and the resulting variations in wood density can make carving difficult. Similarly, broad-leaved trees, which grow very quickly, will show a distinct variation in ring pattern, with soft spring growth and harder bands of late wood. Slow-growing trees generally have more uniform, more narrowly spaced rings,

producing timber of a more even density with which you will achieve better results.

The growth pattern of tropical trees is generally more even than that of trees from temperate zones, as the sun is more consistently overhead and there are fewer seasonal variations of climate. However, habitat has a profound influence on the tree's growth: a tree growing halfway up a mountain in the tropics will experience totally different climatic conditions to a tree at sea level, and will grow accordingly.

This is also true of trees anywhere in the world. For example, an oak down in the far south-west of England will grow more quickly and produce a lower grade of timber than one in, say, Scotland. This is why cold-climate trees need to be differentiated from their temperate-zone cousins. A Scots pine on home ground is one thing, as the cold climate will cause slow growth and produce good carving timber; as an alien in a temperate climate it is quite another matter, and may not be suitable for carving at all. Your timber merchant will be able to help you choose woods from the right climatic source.

Fig 2.3 *Horizontal cross section of tree trunk showing vertical cell structure, medullary rays, and differing annual rings representing spring growth and late wood*

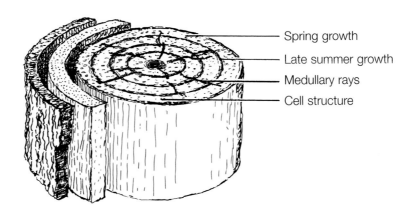

Spring growth
Late summer growth
Medullary rays
Cell structure

Timber conversion

Of the various ways that trees are cut into usable timber, the most common method is to saw the trunk **through and through** into boards (Fig 2.4). These can be of any predetermined thickness, but will usually range from around 1in (25mm) to 4in (100mm). Most relief carving, except very high relief, is carried out using planks, or boards, between 1in (25mm) and 2in (50mm) thick.

Fig 2.5 shows the effect through-and-through (or **flat-sawn**) planking has on the annual-ring configuration. Note that the peripheral planks have the annual rings arcing through their width. But planks from the middle part of the tree's girth have the rings placed nearer to the vertical, as shown in Fig 2.6. This type of wood is said to be **quarter-sawn**.

When the rings lie near to the horizontal (**peripherally cut** planks), they produce circular or flowing grain patterns. But when the rings are closer to the vertical (quarter-sawn or **midway cut**), the grain will be more linear. Figs 2.7 and 2.8 show how the angle of the annual rings affects the appearance of the grain on the top and bottom surfaces.

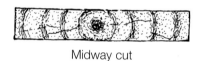

Midway cut

Fig 2.6 *Horizontal cross section through quarter-sawn midway cut*

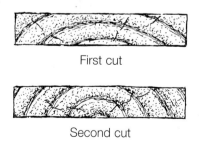

Fig 2.4 *The normal through-and-through planking process, seen here at a small local sawmill*

Plank end

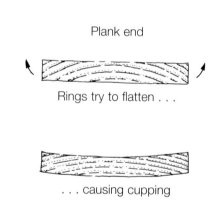

Rings try to flatten . . .

. . . causing cupping

First cut

Second cut

Fig 2.5 *Horizontal cross section of first and second cuts in through-and-through planking, showing annual rings arcing across planks*

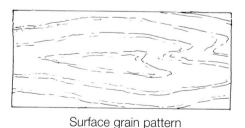

Surface grain pattern

Fig 2.7 *Annual rings in peripherally cut planks, showing the cupping effect and the surface grain pattern produced*

Plank end

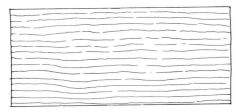

Linear surface grain pattern

Fig 2.8 *Annual rings in quarter-sawn (midway-cut) planks, and the surface grain pattern produced*

Note the upward-pointing arrows in Fig 2.7. These indicate how the wood may distort or cup as the annual rings tend to straighten from an arc to the horizontal. The quarter-sawn wood shown in Fig 2.8 is more stable, but remember that the straighter lines may cause the grain to appear too obtrusive.

To prevent distortion spoiling the look of a carving, it is usual to work with the annual rings pointing upwards, as in Fig 2.9. Then, if there is any distortion, the face of the wood becomes bowed, which is less conspicuous than a cupped surface. A plaque hanging on a wall could tolerate some bowing without its being noticed. Both cupping and bowing are minimized when the board is cut longways down the middle (Fig 2.10).

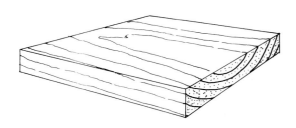

Fig 2.9 *Prevent cupping by working with the annual rings pointing upwards*

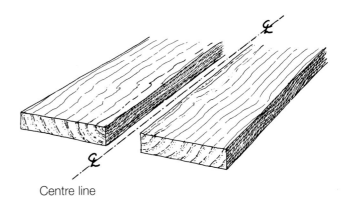

Centre line

Fig 2.10 *Cupping and bowing are minimized by cutting a plank lengthways*

When carving inset panels for furniture – or any item which must retain a flat base, such as a breadboard – always use quarter-sawn timber for the sake of stability. Any visual dominance of the grain lines can usually be reduced by selecting a wood with a bland grain, such as (European) sycamore.

Selecting and buying wood

Buying suitable carving wood, whether home-grown or imported, is fairly straightforward. The best starting point is to look through any of the popular woodworking magazines. They all carry advertisements for stockists. A good supplier will be able to offer boards of a wide range of woods, in a variety of sizes, and will be able to tell you how dry the wood is and how it was seasoned. Later you may wish to buy from a timber yard which keeps stocks of freshly cut wood. You will be able to buy it more cheaply, but you will have to wait a couple of years or more for the wood to season.

Unfortunately, these days not all the wood on offer is of prime quality, and you do need to be selective. Avoid any wood with obvious faults – splits, knots or decay. Trees can have internal splits or **shakes**, caused by storm damage or poor felling (Fig 2.11). These only come to light when the wood is planked. Similar, but more difficult to spot, are shakes which form radially. You may see them

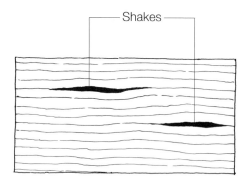

Fig 2.11 *Avoid timber with shakes*

as diagonal lines in the board. Sometimes if you bend the wood across its width they will be visible.

Areas which are pithy will never produce good results. Pithy areas contain soft tissue, and are easy to detect either by sight or by trial cutting. They can be caused by over-rapid growth, or by rot. The most common type of rot is due to fungus, and is generally known as **dote** (Fig 2.12). Fungus stain can penetrate deeply into the wood – look for blotches of darker colour on lime and sycamore, as both these woods are prone to the effects of damp. Similarly, elm suffers from fungus attack if poorly ventilated – look for white powder on the surface. Bad storage can also cause wood surfaces to look stained.

Most beginners try to be far too economical. Be prepared for some wastage. For example, you frequently find board ends have started to split. They might not seem to be very bad, and you could be tempted to ignore them – but don't! Even a tiny split no thicker than a hair's width can quickly open up. Never work right up to the

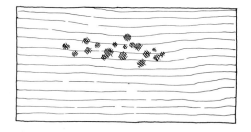

Fig 2.12 *Telltale spots of dote fungus*

original ends: cut back by 2in (50mm) or more and look again (Fig 2.13).

If there is a knot, avoid it. Only seldom will it not detract from or spoil the overall look of your work. Knots shrink, split or even fall out, and the density of the surrounding wood will be different from the rest of the timber.

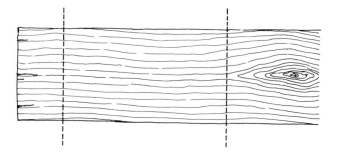

Fig 2.13 *Cut back to avoid end splits and knots*

Seasoning

Before it can be used, timber must be seasoned to reduce its moisture content and lessen the naturally occurring tension present in all growing trees. Seasoning can take place in two main ways – air drying or kiln drying – or a combination of the two.

In the **air-drying** method, cut planks are stacked with spacer sticks in between them; they are said to be **in stick**. The wood is kept in the open and left to dry down to the ambient humidity (Fig 2.14). This takes roughly a year for each inch (25mm) of plank thickness. The slow maturing of the wood means that most, if not all, natural tension is also eliminated.

Generally, air-dried timber carves best, but you should remember that it will only be as dry as the outside humidity. This is always greater than humidity levels in houses, especially those with central heating. Before you use any air-dried wood, it is always a wise precaution to store it for three months or more in a well-ventilated

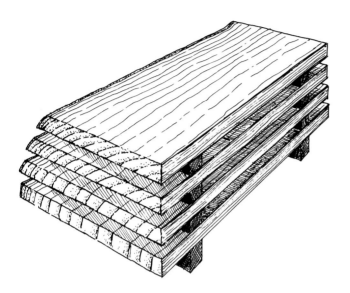

Fig 2.14 *Air-drying timber in stick*

workshop or shed. If you take fresh wood straight into the dry atmosphere of most modern homes, you will be courting trouble.

The old saying 'Grandfather cut down the tree and sawed it into planks, father seasoned it, and his son used it' is certainly very true.

A quicker method for extracting moisture is **kiln-drying**, which relies on controlled dehumidification to produce low levels of retained moisture with little subsequent shrinkage. But the drying processes result in the wood being more brittle and tougher, and is sometimes accompanied by a slight colour change. Not all the natural tension will be released.

Much timber, though, undergoes a combination of the two processes. After air-drying it is reduced to a lower level of moisture content by a short stretch in a kiln. This timber will carve reasonably, but perhaps not quite as well as when just air-dried. However, since there is less risk of shrinkage later on, it can prove suitable for furniture work.

Storage

Store your timber stock in a dry and airy covered place away from direct sunlight. Inside the workshop may be too warm, especially in winter with heating running. Lay the timber on spacer sticks, which should be about 18in (450mm) apart for long planks. The sticks should be around ½in (10mm) square and preferably cut from the same wood, or staining may occur.

As a precaution against splitting, many carvers seal the ends of the boards using either wax or flat oil-based paint. This prevents any remaining moisture drying out too quickly while the wood is stored.

You can get meters to measure the moisture content of wood, but in practice this is not really necessary, especially if you buy supplies from a reliable source. When in doubt, the wood can be weighed at regular intervals to check if it is drying out. But, generally, if you buy sensibly and keep the wood for a reasonable period of time you shouldn't have any problems. You may have to start with kiln-dried stock until your air-dried wood has had time to stabilize.

Figuring and colour

Broadly, the surface figuring you see is made up of annual rings seen lengthwise. But it also has small flecks, which are cells lying at an angle in the wood, and perhaps some medullary rays. All of these will have a visual effect when carved, and need to be taken into account.

Woods vary in colour. The same type of tree grown in differing soil conditions will produce wood of a different shade, due to the effect of minerals and salts in the soil.

Grain

When you look at a piece of wood you don't know which way up it grew, but if you run your hand over the surface you will find one direction is smoother than the other. This shows the lie of the grain (Fig 2.15). Cuts made with the lie of the grain will be shiny, while cuts in the opposite direction will be rough. Wherever possible you should carve with the broad lie of the grain.

Trees which grew straight and tall produce **straight-grained** timber; those which developed in any direction

Fig 2.15 *Feeling the lie of the grain*

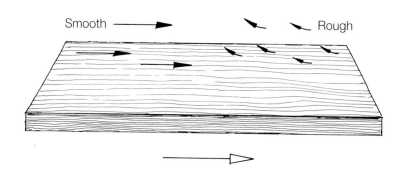

Smooth ⟶   Rough

they pleased usually produce **twisted grain** (Fig 2.16 *a* and *b*). Twisted grain is more difficult to carve, since the direction of cutting has to vary, and the grain effect may not be advantageous. Avoid it if possible.

Some trees spiral as they grow, and when their wood is planked the grain is not uniform in the way it lies. This **interlocked grain** is frequently found in tropical trees. It is always a problem, since it is difficult to cut cleanly. You can recognize interlocked grain because some grain flecks run the length of the wood, while others lie in bands at an angle (Fig 2.17).

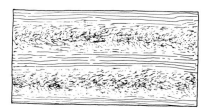

Fig 2.17 *Interlocked grain*

Fitting the wood to the carving

To a great extent the success of a carving can be marred by simply using the wrong wood. Even the most experienced carver would be hard put to produce fine and delicate detail if the timber is just not capable of accepting it; or the subtle lines of a design can be negated by too much colour in the wood. So choosing the right timber for the carving you intend to do is very important, and depends on a combination of scale, detail, and colour and figuring.

● **Scale** is important, because small or delicate carvings require a wood in which the grain will not dominate the design. Strong grain lines, or marked figuring in the wood, are better suited to large or robust work.

● **Detail** in carving is also a consideration – intricate designs necessitate using a close-grained timber. These are generally the types listed as easy or moderately easy to work.

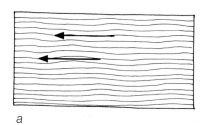

a

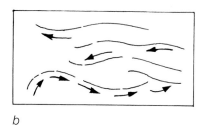

b

Fig 2.16 *Straight grain (a) and twisted grain (b)*

● **Colour and figuring** play a part. Wherever possible it is best to avoid wood which has a pronounced colour variation, as this can detract from the visual effect of the design. Equally, heavily figured wood can present problems if the figuring runs contrary to the direction of the main elements in the carving.

Cell structure

It is also important to know how well the cells in the wood bond to each other, not only individually but also in making up the total growth pattern of the timber. Some woods, like lime, cherry and sycamore, are very stable; their structure is compact, with tiny cells each well bonded to its neighbours. The resultant strength and uniform texture make these woods ideal for carving fine and delicate detail.

In other woods cell size can be larger, and the inter-cell bonding may be weak. While this may not affect the strength of the timber for normal joinery, such weakness will become apparent in delicate carving. Oak is a typical example: though well known for its inherent strength, it has relatively large cells and weak inter-cell bonding. It is consequently difficult to carve oak with fine detail, unless the carver is skilled, as pieces will invariably snap off. Test the strength of cell bonding by trying to break off a small piece from a plank corner with your thumbnail (Fig 2.18). If the wood breaks easily, it has weak inter-cell bonding.

Woods with an interlocked grain can have a sandwich-like appearance in the cell configuration. In some areas the cells will be set longitudinally, while in others they lie

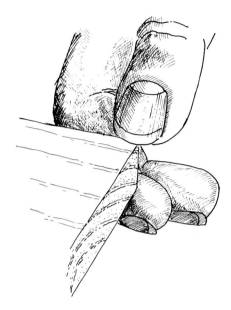

Fig 2.18 *Test wood strength by trying to break off a small corner of the plank*

tangentially to the length of the timber. Bonding will be weak wherever these areas meet. You will often see this in tropical timbers, making them more suited to robust styles of carving.

You will find it helpful to know a couple of technical terms used frequently when describing practical aspects of a carving. **End grain** means any cut surface which exposes the ends of the timber's cells – think of the end of a plank. **Short grain** or **cross grain** refers to elements of a design carved at an angle to the run of the grain – they fall across the path of the grain and the figure pattern on the wood. Fig 2.19 illustrates these terms.

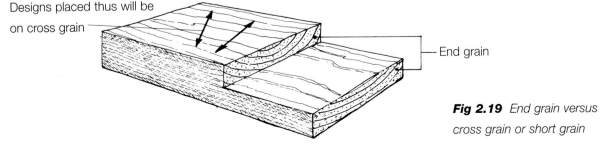

Designs placed thus will be on cross grain

End grain

Fig 2.19 *End grain versus cross grain or short grain*

Suitable carving woods

When considering woods best suited for carving, we are principally interested in slow-growing trees giving wood of an even density, and especially those which produce good-diameter trunks. This will allow planks of a reasonable width – above 6in (150mm) – to be obtained.

Remember, too, that woods with a delicate grain are ideal for working intricate designs, where an obtrusive grain would be totally undesirable. But when the design is fairly bold, woods with a more definite grain pattern can be used. Generally their density will also be greater, and, while somewhat harder to work than woods with a delicate grain, they will produce a more durable polished surface.

Popular European carving woods

LIME (*Tilia vulgaris* or *T. cordata*) Easy to work. Undoubtedly the most suitable wood to start with, lime is known as 'the carver's wood' and is ideal for detailed decoration. The cell structure is very small, and each cell is so well bonded to its neighbour that the chances of the wood fracturing when carved thinly are minimized. It can be straw-coloured or even lighter. The grain is seldom distinctive.

SYCAMORE (*Acer pseudoplatanus*) Varies from easy to moderately difficult to work, depending on the drying method and the length of time it has been seasoned. Slightly harder than lime, but with the same characteristics of small cells, so it takes detail well. It is very light in colour, nearly white in the best grades, but can contain streaks of silver-grey. Grain is subtle, frequently with a ripple pattern. Note that in American usage 'sycamore' refers to a species of plane tree, *Platanus occidentalis*.

CHESTNUT, **sweet** or **Spanish** (*Castanea sativa*) Moderately easy to work. In many respects chestnut resembles flat-sawn oak, but without the medullary rays. Pale brown in colour. The grain is normally straight, but coarse in texture.

ELM (*Ulmus* spp) Difficult to work. This distinctive wood is becoming difficult to obtain in good quality due to the ravages of Dutch elm disease. Of the many types, **English elm** (*Ulmus procera*) is light to dark brown in colour, while **wych elm** (*Ulmus glabra*, also known as **northern elm**) has an attractive green streak to the brown grain.

CHERRY (*Prunus avium*) Moderately easy to work. This is a most attractive wood which takes detail well. Colour is pinkish-brown, sometimes with a green streak. Grain is usually straight.

PEAR (*Pyrus communis*) Difficult to work. Close-grained and quite hard, pear can be ideal for small inset panels in furniture. The wood is strong and tough, but does have a tendency to distort and split. Natural colour is bland, although it takes stain well, but pearwood which has been steamed as part of the seasoning process is pleasingly pink. Even grain and fine texture with little figuring.

WALNUT (*Juglans regia*) Moderately difficult to work, but a delightful wood to carve; well worth its expense. Use with discretion, as its figured grain can either be sympathetic to, or detract from, the design. British walnut is dark brown with much figuring; walnut from France, widely available in the UK, is generally lighter in colour, with a straighter grain. Both are the same species and take fine detail well.

OAK (*Quercus* spp) Difficult to work. Extensively used for ecclesiastical and architectural carving, and still employed today, oak is not a wood to consider until you have built up some expertise, as it is fairly tough and prone to splitting. Colour is light brown, darkening with age; brown oak shows the timber has been attacked by beefsteak fungus, which causes a chemical colour change to take place. Texture is coarse, with large rays.

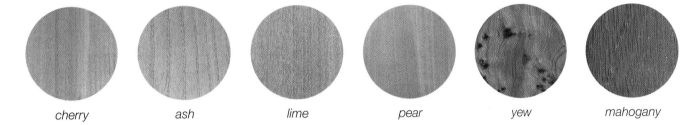

cherry   ash   lime   pear   yew   mahogany

MAHOGANY (*Swietenia* spp) Moderately difficult to work. This is undoubtedly the tropical hardwood most universally used in woodworking generally. There are many species and subspecies, all of which tend to have similar carving properties. It is worth mentioning two important factors. Firstly, while much exquisite carving was carried out in mahogany a hundred years or more ago, it is nowadays impossible to buy new wood of a similar quality – it just doesn't exist. Secondly, there is the moral issue of whether the timber available today is ecologically sustainable. Many woodworkers are, for this reason alone, turning away completely from the use of tropical hardwoods; others try to ensure their supplies come from renewable sources. You could try to find some reclaimed material – old and broken pieces of furniture can easily make suitable carving wood.

SCOTS PINE (*Pinus sylvestris*) Moderately difficult to work. Classified as a softwood. Also known as **redwood**, the better Scots pine is widely distributed throughout the colder parts of Europe, especially Scandinavia. Colour is light brown. Though it cuts reasonably easily, the wood is prone to knots and you should expect some density variation.

YEW (*Taxus baccata*) Difficult to work. Despite its botanical classification as a softwood, this is a tough timber. It is very hard, but can be used effectively for small carvings – though you should expect a high element of wastage from knots, holes and ingrowing bark. Colour varies from light to rich brown, with purple tints which fade with exposure to daylight. Usually has a 'wild' grain.

ASH (*Fraxinus excelsior*) Moderately easy to work. Can be prone to splitting, making it unsuitable for fine detail. Generally pale or almost white in colour, but can have brown heartwood. Old trees of large girth can produce a mass of even figuring at right angles to the grain, which is known as **olive ash** or **ripple ash**. The ripple often has treacle-coloured streaks.

Popular American carving woods

BASSWOOD (*Tilia americana*) Easy to work. Also known as **American lime**, basswood is similar to its European cousin and shares the same carving properties. Colour is creamy-white, sometimes pale brown. Straight grain and even texture.

BUTTERNUT (*Juglans cinerea*) Moderately difficult to work. Also known as **white walnut**, butternut is difficult to obtain in Britain. The wood displays most of the characteristics of walnut and has similar grain patterns, but is lighter in colour. Expect some wastage.

CHERRY (*Prunus serotina*) Moderately difficult to work. The wood has good working properties, and is reddish-brown in colour. Fine grain and even texture.

RED OAK (*Quercus rubra* or *Q. falcata*) Moderately difficult to work. **Northern red oak** (*Q. rubra*) is considered by many carvers to be superior. Colour is biscuit-pink to brown. Open grain.

BLACK WALNUT (*Juglans nigra*) Difficult to work. This wood needs to be worked with care for fine detail.

It is richly coloured, varying from dark brown to almost black. Grain verges on coarse, and is usually straight but sometimes wavy.

WESTERN WHITE PINE (*Pinus monticola*) Moderately easy to work. The heartwood is a pale straw colour, only slightly darker than the sapwood. It is straight-grained with an even texture.

Popular Australian carving woods

HOOP PINE (*Araucaria cunninghamii*) Easy to work. The heartwood is yellow-brown to darker brown with a pinkish cast. It is straight-grained with a uniform and fine texture.

HUON PINE (*Dacrydium franklinii*) Easy to work. The heartwood is a pale yellow. The sapwood is undefined. Grain is straight and of even texture.

ALPINE ASH (*Eucalyptus delegatensis*) Moderately difficult to work. The colour varies from pale to light brown with a pinkish tinge. It is straight-grained with an open texture. Occasionally has interlocked or wavy grain.

BLACK BEAN (*Castanospermum australe*) Difficult to work. The heartwood is chocolate-brown, figured with grey-brown streaks. It is generally straight-grained though sometimes interlocked. Its texture is rather coarse.

JARRAH (*Eucalyptus marginata*) Difficult to work. The heartwood is light to dark red, and often has darker markings or speckles. The sapwood is pale yellow to off-white. Its grain is slightly interlocked and is of a coarse, even texture.

Summary

- Select only good-quality wood.

- Take advice from a reputable timber supplier.

- Store your stock with care, and with due regard to ventilation and temperature.

- Match the wood to the planned carving in respect of grain, colour and texture. If any of these is too dominant it can spoil the look of your work.

- Always treat your wood with respect. It may have taken 150 years to grow; you can ruin it in as many minutes.

3 selecting carving tools

When you first look at the range of woodcarving tools available, it can seem bewildering. There are so many different shapes and sizes to choose from, so how do you start to make your selection? Happily, all differences between woodcarving tools boil down to three main distinctions:

1 the shape of the tool when viewed from head on
2 the shape of the tool when viewed from the side
3 the shape of the tool when viewed from above.

Blade shape: The head-on view

Fig 3.1 represents the head-on view of the most common woodcarving tools. It can easily be seen that all the tools are one of three basic shapes: a perfectly straight line (nos. 1 and 2), a curve (nos. 3–11), or a V-shape (nos. 45, 39 and 41). There are a few specialized tools, such as the macaroni, whose end shapes do not fit neatly into this classification scheme. It would be rare to find a use for such a tool unless, perhaps, you were restoring antique furniture.

● **Chisels and skews** A tool whose head-on shape is a straight line is either a **chisel** (no. 1) or a **skew** (no. 2). No. 2 in Fig 3.1 actually shows the shape of the skew as it would be seen from the top. This view shows that, although the head-on view of the skew is identical to that of the chisel – that is, a straight line – it is distinguished from the chisel by having its cutting edge at an angle.

Chisels are straight-bladed tools with a bevel on both sides, and are used for straight cuts. Chisels are also used to smooth carved surfaces. Skews are quite useful for the woodcarver, especially for undercutting and for cleaning out corners. If you are just starting out and need to choose one or the other, choose the skew. You will find it more versatile.

● **Gouges** form the largest group of woodcarving tools. Gouges are those tools whose shape, when viewed from head on, is a curve (Fig 3.2). The gouges are distinguished from each other, aside from variances in size, by the

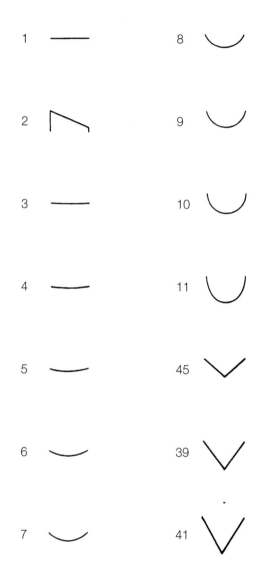

1 ——

8 ⌣

2

9 ⌣

3 ——

10 ⌣

4 ——

11 ⌣

5 ——

45 ∨

6 ⌣

39 ∨

7 ⌣

41 ∨

Fig 3.1 *Blade shapes of straight tools, with their Sheffield List numbers (by courtesy of Henry Taylor (Tools) Ltd)*

degree of curvature each displays. Nos. 3–9 of Fig 3.1 are true arcs of a circle; no. 9 is a half-circle (Figs 3.3 and 3.4). Nos. 10 and 11 have deep sides, which gives the end view of these tools a U-shape; they are not true arcs of a circle.

Gouges have a bevel ground on the back of the blade. When the gouge is pushed into the wood, either by hand pressure or by a blow from a mallet, the blade slices cleanly through the wood fibres and maintains a constant

level of cut until pressure is let up. The bevel then forces the blade out again, leaving a smooth, spoon-shaped depression. Gouges are very efficient at removing large quantities of wood. Moreover, if the tool is very sharp and the bevel is polished, the metal of the tool actually burnishes the surface of the wood as it cuts, providing you are cutting with the grain.

Fig 3.2 *Three basic blades: typical English-type gouges nos. 3, 7 and 9*

Fig 3.3 *Gouges nos. 3 and 5*

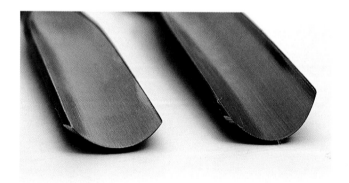

Fig 3.4 *Gouges nos. 7 and 9*

● **Veiners and fluters** (nos. 10 and 11 of Fig 3.1) are merely gouges with U-shaped cutting edges (Fig 3.5). Their deeper sides and U-shape make them useful for grooving, outlining, and hollowing out surfaces. The smaller of the U-shaped tools are called **veiners**, the larger, **fluters**, because they were traditionally used to carve the veins and flutes of acanthus foliage.

● **V-tools or parting tools** (nos. 39–45 of Fig 3.1) have a distinctive V-shape when viewed from head on. They are normally available with the V in angles of approximately 45°, 60° and 90°. Fig 3.6 shows a V-tool with a 60° angle. V-tools do a great deal of the carving in incised work.

● **Sizes of woodcarving tools** Fig 3.7 indicates the great range of sizes in which woodcarving gouges are offered. The size of woodcarving tools is described by the width of the cutting edge, measured from tip to tip. Measurements are given either in imperial measurements or metric, depending on the manufacturer. Most manufacturers offer sizes ranging from 1⁄16in (1.5mm) to 1in (25mm), but larger sizes can be found.

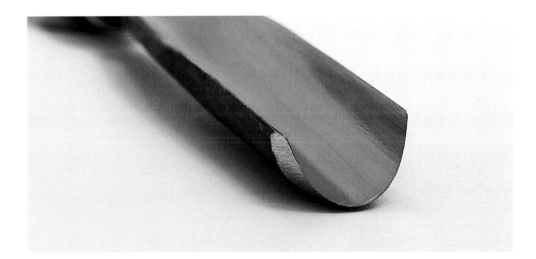

Fig 3.5 *Gouge no. 11*

Fig 3.6 *V-tool no. 39 with nominal 60° angle*

FULL RANGE OF SWEEPS AND SIZES					$\frac{1}{16}$ 1.5	$\frac{3}{32}$ 2.25	$\frac{1}{8}$ 3	$\frac{3}{16}$ 4.5
London Pattern straight gouges	London Pattern curved gouges	London Pattern spoonbit gouges (frontbent)	London Pattern spoonbit gouges (backbent)	Fishtail pattern straight gouges				
3	12	24	33	54 x 3	–	–	‿	‿
4	13	25	34	54 x 4	–	–	‿	‿
5	14	26	35	54 x 5	–	‿	‿	‿
6	15	27	36	54 x 6	‿	‿	‿	‿
7	16	28	37	54 x 7	‿	‿	‿	‿
8	17	29	38	54 x 8	‿	‿	‿	‿
9	18	30	–	54 x 9	‿	‿	‿	‿
10	19	31	–	54 x 10	‿	‿	‿	‿
11	20	32	–	54 x 11	‿	‿	‿	‿

Fig 3.7 (above) *London Pattern range of gouge sweeps and sizes (by courtesy of Ashley Iles (Edge Tools) Ltd)*

Blade shape: The side view

When viewed from the side, the blades of woodcarving tools can be either straight or bent (Fig 3.8). The bent tools follow three main styles: curved (4 in Fig 3.8), frontbent (5–8) and backbent (12). **Straight** tools are the most often used tools, and are used for all ordinary work.

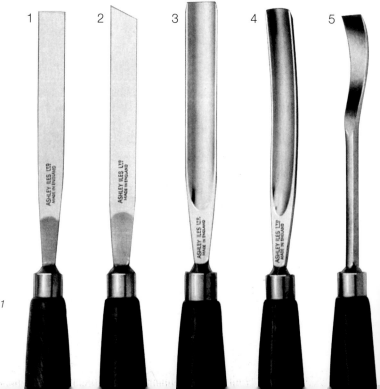

1	Straight chisel no. 1	8	Spoon gouge, frontbent nos. 24–32
2	Straight corner (skew) chisel no. 2	9	V-tool nos. 39–46
3	Straight gouge nos. 3–11	10	Grounding tool no. 47 x 3
4	Curved gouge nos. 12–20	11	Dogleg chisel no. 52
5	Spoon chisel no. 21	12	Spoon gouge, backbent nos. 33–38
6	Spoon chisel, left corner no. 22	13	Fishtail gouge no. 54 x 3–11
7	Spoon chisel, right corner no. 23	14	Fishtail chisel no. 54 x 1–2

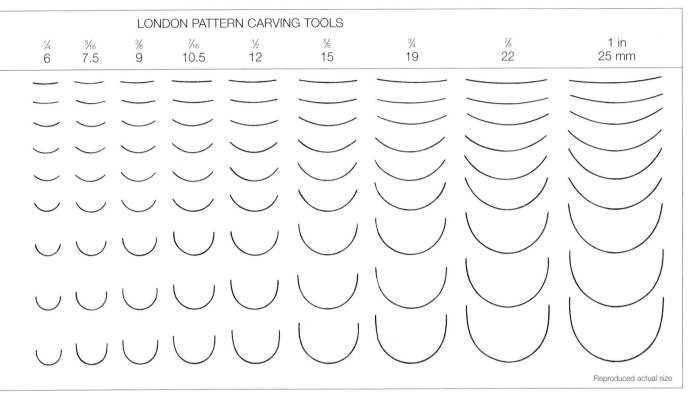

LONDON PATTERN CARVING TOOLS								
¼ 6	⁵⁄₁₆ 7.5	⅜ 9	⁷⁄₁₆ 10.5	½ 12	⅝ 15	¾ 19	⅞ 22	1 in 25 mm

Reproduced actual size

Fig 3.8 (below) *Range of standard London Pattern carving tools (by courtesy of Ashley Iles (Edge Tools) Ltd)*

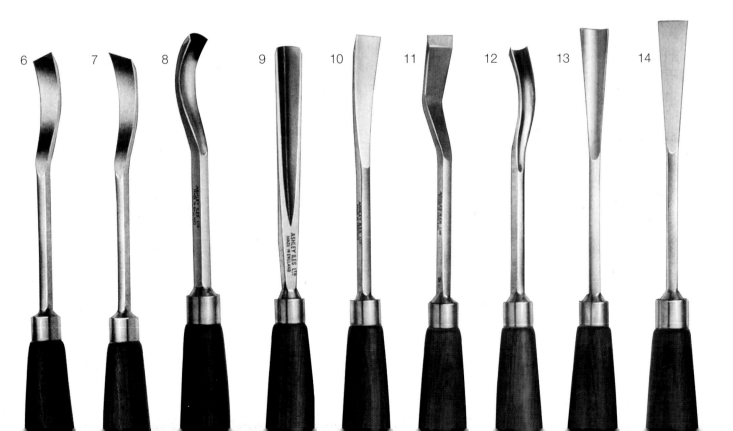

6   7   8   9   10   11   12   13   14

Fig 3.9 Frontbent (at rear) and backbent spoon gouges

Curved tools are used for working shallow hollows. **Frontbent** or **spoonbit** tools, whose longitudinal shape has a shorter, more abrupt curve, are used for working in deeper hollows. **Backbent** tools are used to work convex surfaces (Fig 3.9).

The **dogleg chisel** (11 in Fig 3.8) is an exception to the three common bends seen in tool blades. The dogleg chisel finds quite a bit of use, especially in cleaning up recessed areas and in deep undercutting. The bent design allows the cutting edge of the tool access to hard-to-reach areas.

Blade shape: The top view

When viewed from the top, the blades of gouges can be seen to vary in shape. Basic gouges have sides that are parallel from the cutting edge to where the handle normally begins. These gouges are recommended for the beginner. They readily accept a blow from the mallet. Moreover, when such a gouge is reground, the shape and size of its cutting edge are maintained. Gouges with parallel sides will last through many regrindings.

Other gouges, when viewed from above, will be seen to taper, to a greater or lesser degree, toward the tang (again see Fig 3.8). The **fishtail**, whether it be a fishtail gouge (13) or a fishtail chisel (14), exhibits a dramatic taper from the cutting edge to the tang (Fig 3.10). This taper, or wasting away of the metal, weakens the tool. However, because there is less metal behind the cutting edge, these tools can be used in areas where the straight side of a basic gouge would knock or scrape against the work, fouling it. Moreover, the taper allows for greater visibility.

Besides a loss of blade strength, the main disadvantage of tapered tools is that they lose their shape and size upon being reground.

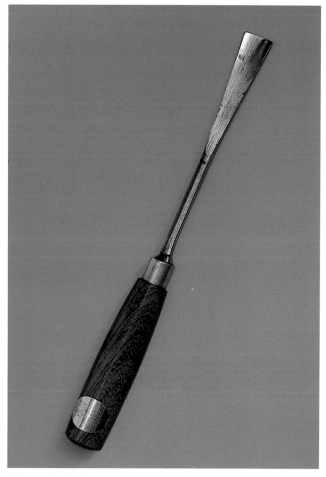

Fig 3.10 Fishtail gouge, 54 x 3

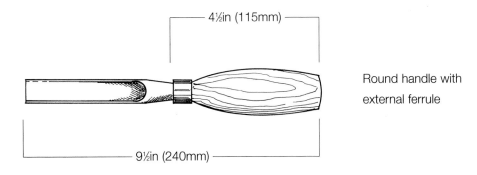

Fig 3.11 *Typical English short-handled carving tool*

4½in (115mm)

Round handle with external ferrule

9½in (240mm)

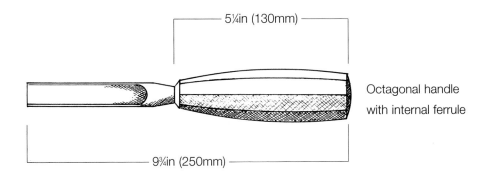

Fig 3.12 *Swiss-style gouge, with long octagonal handle*

5¼in (130mm)

Octagonal handle with internal ferrule

9¾in (250mm)

Handles

The shape of the English carving tool evolved centuries ago, and was primarily determined by the hardness of the oak traditionally used for much of the work (such as you generally find in old churches, for example), and the need to carry out most of the carving using a mallet. These factors dictated a relatively short carving tool, and a handle reinforced with a brass ferrule. Most English gouges have an overall length and handle shape similar to the one shown in Fig 3.11.

Swiss carving tools, which have become very popular in recent years, probably evolved because European carvers traditionally worked in woods softer than oak. Their style of carving relied mainly on hand pressure to power the gouge, with little use of a mallet, and a longer handle was favoured. Continental carvers also adopted an octagonal handle shape (Fig 3.12), usually with an internal reinforcing sleeve.

It is interesting to note that as softer woods became fashionable, English carvers started to adopt longer and differently shaped handles. About one hundred years ago 5in (125mm) handles were common, with shapes such as those shown in Fig 3.13.

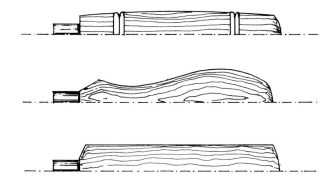

Fig 3.13 *Variations in shape found in older handles*

It is very much a matter of personal taste whether you buy the English or Swiss style of carving gouge. While the longer Swiss types are ideal for hand carving, many people prefer the London Pattern (English) gouge for mallet work, as the shorter length is easier to control.

Handle comfort is also an important factor: some people find the octagonal shape comfortable to use, others do not. Octagonal handles prevent tools from rolling off the work table so easily, and so can prevent them from being damaged.

If you have the opportunity, try handling both types and find out how they feel in use, then buy the type you like best. There is nothing wrong with mixing the styles, of course – I have almost a hundred gouges, of which some are Swiss and some London Pattern, some are old and some new.

The Swiss numbering system (shown in part in Fig 3.14) differs somewhat from the Sheffield List numbers, mainly in the shallower-cutting gouges. The Swiss no. 5, for example, is nearer to an English no. 4; their no. 7 is more like an English no. 5.

Some manufacturers offer standard-size tools as well as shorter ('junior' or 'amateur') versions. There is no merit at all in buying the shorter versions. Similarly, the very small lino-cutting types are not worth buying – the steel is seldom tempered, so they will never be able to hold a keen cutting edge.

A word about tool patterns

Over the years generations of woodcarvers have established the size and shape of tools needed, for everything from the most basic cuts through to intricate

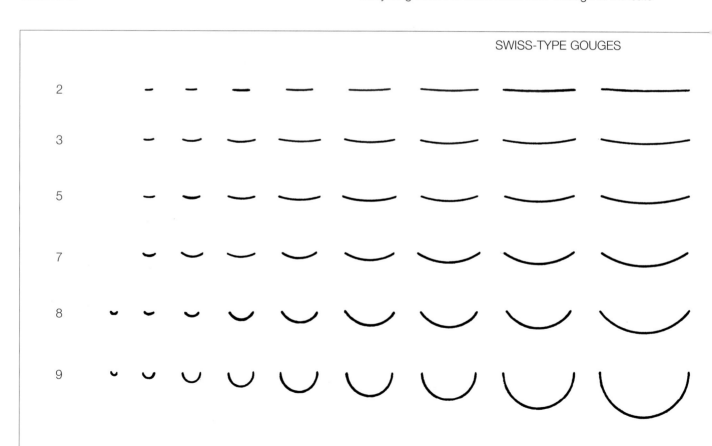

Fig 3.14 Swiss gouge numbering chart (by courtesy of Craft Supplies Ltd)

and detailed work. The range of patterns became standardized about a hundred years ago. Most British tool manufacturers were based in Sheffield, so the patterns were formulated into what came to be known as the Sheffield List. This list included all the actual shapes needed, and gave them a uniform numbering system which is still used today.

You will also come across references to London Pattern carving tools. This term arose originally because, while most of the tools were made in Sheffield, a great deal of the actual carving was done in London. However, for all practical purposes the descriptions are one and the same, and you get the normal English-style carving tool. Unless otherwise stated, the numbering used in this book (including the London Pattern numbering in Fig 3.7, page 28) is that of the Sheffield List.

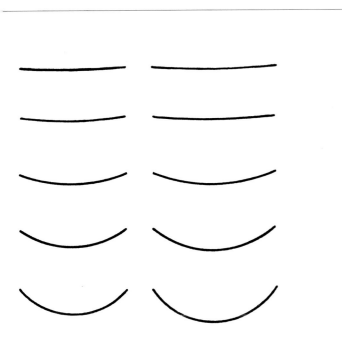

This partial chart shows how the Swiss numbering differs from the London Pattern. Sizes are measured in mm from tip to tip. Reproduced actual size

Selecting your first tools

The size and shape of the tools you need are governed by the type and scale of the carving being undertaken. This is why most experienced carvers end up with a vast array of tools, but for anyone just starting out a more moderate number will suffice. Indeed, it can become quite confusing if one's choice is initially too great, so buy a few tools to start with and build up as you gain more experience.

Most manufacturers offer boxed sets of tools, but because the size of a carving dictates to a great degree the size of the tool used, a boxed set may contain one or two tools you would never use. It makes more sense to buy tools individually.

For a normal size of work (anything up to about 18 x 12in or 450 x 300mm, say), a suitable first choice of tools for beginners would be:

- ⅜in (9mm) no. 2 skew chisel
- *¼in (6mm) no. 3 gouge
- ⅝in (15mm) no. 3 gouge
- *⅜in (9mm) no. 4 gouge
- *⅜in (9mm) no. 5 gouge
- ½in (12mm) no. 6 gouge
- *¼in (6mm) no. 9 gouge
- *⅟₁₆in (1.5mm) no. 11 veiner
- ¼in (6mm) no. 39 60° V-tool

The ones marked with an asterisk are the basic minimum tools required to start carving. If you plan to produce carvings larger than average size, you may need to obtain some of these tools in increased blade widths.

As you gain more experience, the following additions would be useful:

- ½in (12mm) no. 1 chisel
- ⅝in (15mm) no. 4 gouge
- ½in (12mm) no. 9 gouge
- ¼in (6mm) no. 11 veiner
- ½in (12mm) no. 15 curved gouge
- ¼in (6mm) no. 28 frontbent spoonbit

All these numbers refer to London Pattern tools: for their Swiss equivalents, look at the chart of Swiss carving tools (Fig 3.14, previous page) and cross-refer to the London Pattern chart (Fig 3.7, page 28).

A ¼in (6mm) no. 47 grounding tool (only made by Ashley Iles) is a very useful gouge for tidying up the background of relief carvings. Another tool which is very effective when working small areas of detail is a no. 52 dogleg chisel.

Where to buy tools

Collecting, and using, old tools has become very popular – there are now quite a few specialist retail shops selling only old tools. Certainly these outlets can be useful if you are looking for a special size or shape of gouge, particularly one which may not even be made these days. Many people also hold the view that the quality of workmanship of old tools is superior. Two famous makes worth looking out for are Herring and Addis.

Some makers factory-sharpen their tools, others do not. Clearly, from the beginner's point of view, it makes sense to buy the pre-sharpened types. The English firm Ashley Iles and the Swiss maker Pfeil come into this category. But it is important to realize that a gouge or chisel will not stay sharp – really sharp – for very long. You need to know how to keep your tools in razor-sharp condition. Full details concerning the methods for sharpening various tools, as well as the equipment needed, are provided in Chapter 4. I mention this now because you may prefer to buy a make which is not factory-sharpened, such as Henry Taylor's Acorn Brand.

Mallets

Even if you plan to do most carving initially with just hand pressure, a mallet will undoubtedly be needed from time to time, and especially when waste wood has to be removed. Carving mallets have round heads and short handles (Fig 3.15). It isn't really possible to use the

conventional carpenter's type, because the round head of the carver's mallet is designed so it doesn't deflect the cutting line of the gouge if it is hit slightly off-centre. Also, the short handle is more comfortable to use, the hitting action coming from the forearm with the wrist locked.

Generally, mallets are made from beech or lignum vitae. The latter, being made from a denser wood, are heavier than beech ones of a similar size. But lignum vitae is now a rare wood, and there are alternatives made from sustainable timber. The manufacturing process for these employs resin-bonded laminations to produce a heavy, dense material with similar characteristics to lignum vitae. Whatever type of mallet you buy, though, it must have an impact-absorbing handle – ash is frequently used for this purpose. A beech mallet around 3½in (90mm) diameter will be sufficient to begin with.

Fig 3.15 *A typical carver's mallet*

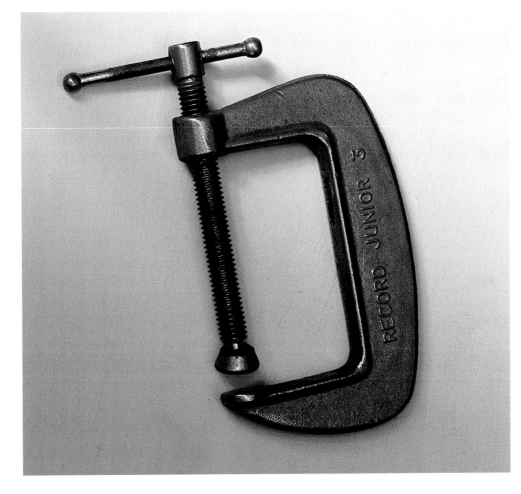

Fig 3.16 G-clamp for holding work securely

Clamps

There are various ways of holding the wood securely, but if you are starting from scratch a simple G-clamp (C-clamp) is easy to use and cheap to buy (Fig 3.16). You will need two: those with a 6in (150mm) gape will be more than adequate. For further information on holding work, see Chapter 5.

Apart from the equipment needed for keeping your tools sharp (see Chapter 4), we have now covered the basic requirements for carving wood. Other tools may be needed for the projects, but these will be items generally used for woodworking, and their need will be obvious at the time. Store carving tools in a purpose-made tool roll to protect cutting edges from damage.

Summary

● **Only buy good-quality tools.**

● **Store your gouges and chisels in a tool roll to protect their cutting edges.**

● **Avoid boxed sets and buy your tools individually. Start with a small number, then build up as you gain experience.**

● **Look out for old makes, such as Addis and Herring.**

4 tool sharpening

To produce a perfect carving, your tools must be razor-sharp. A relief carving relies for its effectiveness on light reflecting off the cut surfaces, and only sharp tools will create a really reflective surface. Cuts produced by blunt tools need extensive sanding, which leaves the carving looking dull and flat.

If you buy factory-sharpened tools you will be able to carve for a time before they need attention, and then only stropping may be required. However, sooner or later you will need to know more about sharpening the cutting edge. If your tools are not pre-sharpened, you will have to master the technique before you can begin carving.

A common mistake among beginners is failing to keep their tools really sharp because they are simply unaware that the edges are blunting. But in time, with experience, this can be felt. A cutting edge needs to be touched up by stropping frequently, perhaps as often as every ten minutes if the wood is hard – just as, say, a player chalks the tip of a snooker or pool cue. If you neglect this, the result of hours of labour will be as if the dog has had a good chew at the wood.

Bevels

When you know how to do it, each stage of sharpening is quite straightforward: stropping the cutting edge to keep it razor-sharp, honing the bevel to form the cutting edge, and perhaps once in a while regrinding the tool. To understand each process, it is helpful to know something about bevels in general.

Bevels are needed to bring the relative thickness of the blade to a thin cutting edge. The main bevel is on the outside of the gouge, which helps to control the depth of cut (Fig 4.1), although additional bevels can also be formed (see Fig 4.5a on page 38). This is the fundamental difference between a carving gouge and a carpenter's scribing or paring gouge – the latter has the bevel on the inside of the blade (Fig 4.2). Carving *chisels* have two equal bevels, one on each side of the blade (Fig 4.3).

The angle of the bevel is important, as it dictates the angle of cut (Fig 4.4). If it is ground too shallow (say, below 15°) the blade tip will be too thin

Fig 4.1 Carvers' gouges
have the main cutting bevel
on the outside of the blade

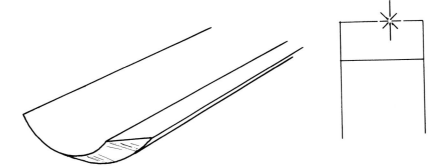

for practical use. If it is ground too steeply, entry of the tool into the wood will be difficult.

Many people new to carving experience difficulty in understanding what constitutes a correct bevel angle. Perhaps this stems from the belief that in any range of tools the bevels should always be at the same angle; a belief reinforced by the fact that tool makers invariably grind all their tools with similar bevels. If you've just bought some tools, have a look – you will almost certainly find they all have similar bevels.

While factory-set bevels are often perfectly satisfactory to start with, you may wish to know more about bevel angles. In fact, the angle of the bevel should be determined by how the tool will be used. If a gouge is going to be used for working hard and tough wood, such as oak, powered by quite heavy mallet blows, the cutting edge will need to be strong. This means having a relatively short bevel with a steep angle. But if the gouge will be used on softer woods, or by hand for taking light cuts, then a lower angle of entry will be required, so you need a shallow bevel.

Years ago it was traditional to use a 40° angle for hard and dense woods, reducing the bevel to around 30° for

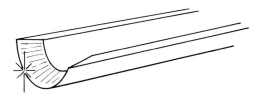

Fig 4.2 Some carpenters' gouges have an inside bevel, but no bevel on the outside

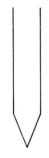

Fig 4.3 A carving chisel has two bevels

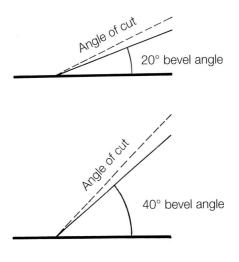

Fig 4.4 The bevel controls the minimum angle of cut

softer and more easily worked timber. It was also common practice for carvers to sharpen their gouges with a narrow leading bevel set at a steeper angle than the main bevel (Fig 4.5a). Even today, this arrangement has much to commend it for gouges used for a lot of hard work, such as removing waste wood. Apart from the advantage of added strength, it gives control to the tool by allowing it to pivot at the point where the two bevels meet.

These days many carvers opt to use a single 20° outside bevel (Fig 4.5b), which can be sharpened easily both with mechanical systems and with oilstones. However, a small bevel can still be formed on the inside of the gouge, bringing the cutting edge nearer to the centre of the blade's thickness. This can be useful for strong tools with relatively thick blades, and has two other advantages. Firstly, when clearing away waste wood the steeper angle of the inside bevel makes chips tend to curl up and snap off more easily; secondly, it provides a better cutting point when a tool has to be used inverted, such as when carving round shapes like berries or nuts (Fig 4.6). You will find it useful to include an inside bevel on the flatter gouges.

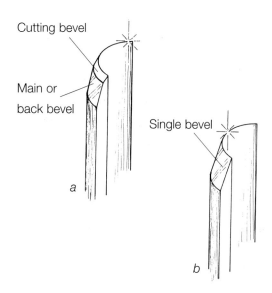

Fig 4.5 (a) Traditional two-bevel edge
(b) Single, or continuous, bevel setting

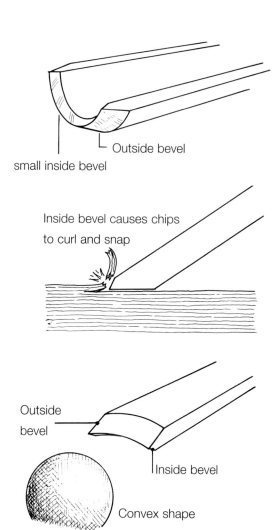

Fig 4.6 It can be useful to have a small inside bevel, especially when using the gouge inverted to carve convex shapes such as berries. The inside bevel also causes chips to curl and snap off easily

Oilstones

For generations carvers have used **oilstones** (also known as **benchstones**) for honing their cutting edges. A more recent introduction is the Japanese waterstone, which works on the same principle as the oilstone but has to be kept permanently wet. Waterstones are also soft, and wear quickly into grooves. I prefer oilstones, so I shall concentrate on these (Fig 4.7).

Fig 4.7 A standard
oilstone in its box

There are two basic types of oilstone: man-made
and natural. Man-made 'India' combination stones have
a coarse grade on one side and a medium grade on the
other. They are fairly inexpensive and work reasonably
well. The superior type, and a better investment in the
long run, is the 'Arkansas' stone. These are natural hard
stones available in medium, fine and very fine grades. You
can buy individual stones of one grade, or combination
types. The individual stones are better, as you can use
one side for gouges, which may cause grooves, and keep
the other side for flat chisels.

Oilstones are lubricated with light oil, to prevent traces
of metal becoming embedded in the surface. Thin the oil
with a small amount of paraffin (kerosene) if necessary.

Honing a single-bevel gouge

If you are right-handed, follow these instructions; for
left-handed operation, reverse the hands.

Apply a few drops of oil to the stone. Use the
lubricated oilstone sideways on. Hold the gouge in your
right hand with the index finger along the top of the blade

(Fig 4.8). Let the bevel rest on the surface of the stone.
Position the left index and second fingers low down on
the blade (Fig 4.9).

Use the left hand both to press down and to provide
side-to-side motion across the stone. At the same time
rotate the gouge with the right hand so that all the sweep
comes into contact. You need to reach each corner of
the blade (Fig 4.10), but do not twist beyond the corners
or you will distort the shape of the cutting edge. Some
carvers prefer to adopt a figure-of-eight motion instead of
just side-to-side sweeping strokes (Fig 4.11). Maintain the
gouge angle continually and consistently – avoid letting
the handle drop at any time.

After a few strokes check for roughness on the inside
of the cutting edge, which indicates when you have
sharpened to the very edge of the blade. This roughness,
known as the **rag** or **burr**, is taken off with a slipstone
(see pages 45–6).

If you haven't achieved this burr, make sure that
you are applying sufficient downward pressure with your
left-hand fingers, and that you are keeping the bevel

Fig 4.8 *Using an oilstone: position of the right hand*

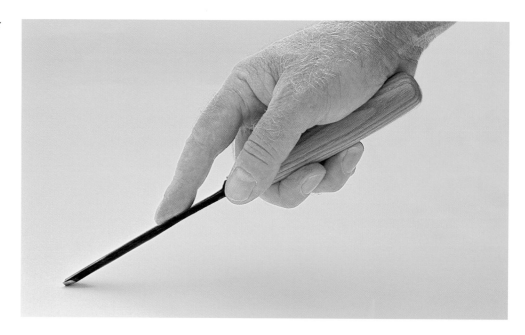

Fig 4.9 *Using an oilstone: position of the left hand*

constantly in full contact with the oilstone. If you have a tendency to lower the handle at all when the gouge is gliding across the stone, this will cause the cutting edge to lift. Alternatively, you may have been holding the tool at too shallow an angle for the edge to contact the stone. The burr is a must.

Honing a two-bevel gouge

If you want to form a secondary bevel, the procedure is just the same as for honing a single bevel, except that after resting the main bevel on the stone the handle must be raised so as to bring only the edge of the blade tip into contact.

Fig 4.10 *Getting to the corner of the blade*

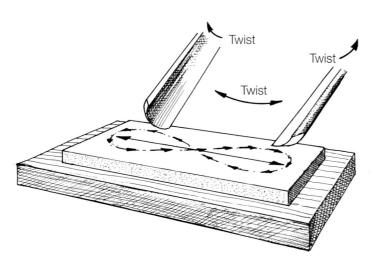

Twist

Twist

Twist

Fig 4.11 *Using a side-to-side or a figure-of-eight movement to cover the full sweep of the gouge*

Before you start, experiment by laying the main bevel on the lubricated surface of the oilstone. Then gently raise the handle until you see the oil beginning to bubble up onto the tip of the blade. The bubbling is very slight, but it shows that only the edge of the gouge is resting on the oilstone. Note the angle at which you are holding the gouge, and keep to this angle while you hone the leading bevel (Fig 4.12).

When carried out correctly the cutting bevel should not be more than ⅟₁₆in (1.5mm) wide, and its width must be equal across the sweep of the blade. Check that it does not widen at any point, which indicates either that unequal downward pressure is being applied, or that the amount of blade rotation is insufficient. Either or both will cause undue wear, and make the cutting edge become misshapen.

Fig 4.12 *Honing a two-bevel gouge, with the blade at a higher angle than for a single-bevel gouge* (shown inset)

Honing chisels

Chisels are honed using the oilstone lengthways on, making a forward stroke (never backward strokes, to avoid rounding the bevel). Use an equal number of strokes on each side of the blade to ensure the cutting edge remains in the middle. As with gouges, the angle must be kept constant throughout the stroke (Fig 4.13). Avoid letting the handle dip to any extent towards the end of the stroke, as this will tend to round the bevel too much.

Honing the V-tool

Sharpen the V-tool in the same manner as for a chisel, using an equal number of strokes on each blade of the V. Then turn the oilstone sideways and rotate the underside of the tool where the two blades meet. This area should be slightly rounded like a gouge – *not* like a knife edge – and rounding on an oilstone will remove any small 'hook' that may form at the intersection of the two blades (Fig 4.14).

Fig 4.13 *Honing a chisel, with the blade at a low angle. An angle as low as 10–15° might be preferred for delicate work in lime*

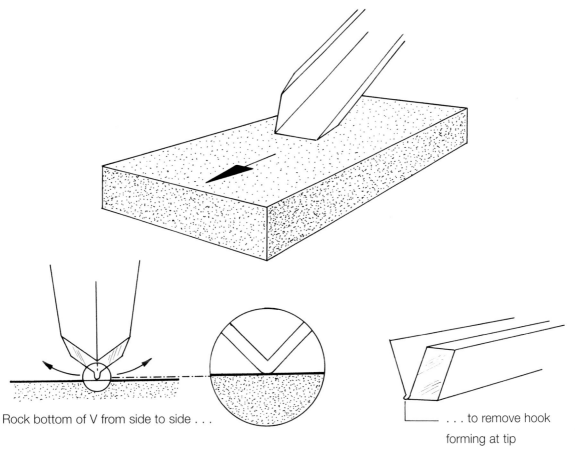

Rock bottom of V from side to side . . .

. . . to remove hook forming at tip

Fig 4.14 *When honing a V-tool, rock the bottom of the V from side to side to remove the hook forming at the tip, and to give the tool a slightly rounded base rather than a razor-sharp angle*

Honing the veiner

Veiners (U-shaped gouges) have a reputation for being difficult to sharpen. They are certainly more difficult than ordinary gouges, but should not really cause you any problems. Veiners *can* be honed in the same way as a single-bevel gouge, but this may cause the sides to become too worn because of the veiner's U-shaped cross section (Fig 4.15). For this reason they are easier to hone if you use the oilstone lengthways, as when sharpening a

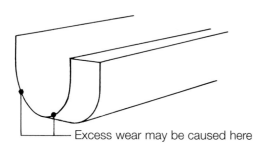

Excess wear may be caused here

Fig 4.15 *Honing a veiner like an ordinary gouge can cause undue wear on the sides of the U*

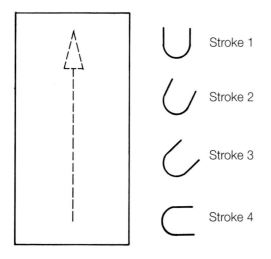

Stroke 1

Stroke 2

Stroke 3

Stroke 4

Fig 4.16 *Use a forward stroke down the length of the oilstone, rotating one side of the veiner. Repeat for the other side*

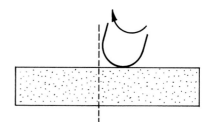

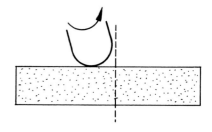

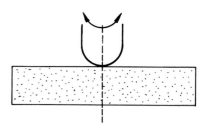

Fig 4.17 *The alternative method of honing a veiner is to work each side from the U-bend, then finish with a few strokes across the bottom of the blade*

chisel. You must rotate the veiner so that all the sweep comes into contact with the oilstone, and avoid excessive pressure (Fig 4.16).

Alternatively, use the gouge honing sequence, but do it in three parts. Starting from an off-centre position, where the bottom curve joins the side walls, hone each side in turn using an equal number of strokes. Then finish off by sharpening the bottom of the U as you would a gouge (Fig 4.17).

Last but not least, if V-tools and veiners are kept well stropped there will be virtually no need to use an oilstone.

Using slipstones

Slipstones or **slips** are made from the same material as oilstones, and again the Arkansas types are the better buy (Fig 4.18). They are used to remove the rough **burr**, or **rag**, left on the inside of the blade when the cutting edge has been honed correctly; and also to form inside bevels.

There are two ways the burr can be removed, and in each case you need a slipstone of a size to suit the inside sweep of the gouge. You will only need a few slips, perhaps two or three, as the faces of the stones are tapered to provide edges with differing radii. Arkansas types are normally sold in sets.

If you choose to have an inside bevel, hold the blade firmly against the edge of the bench top. With the side of the slipstone lubricated with a few drops of oil, rub it against the inside edge of the gouge at an angle of about 15°. After a few strokes back and forth you will find the rough burr has been removed and a small bevel formed (Fig 4.19).

Fig 4.18 *An India slipstone*

If you don't want the inner bevel, keep the slipstone flat against the inside of the gouge (Fig 4.20).

Although triangular slips are made for V-tools, manufacturing tolerances are such that they are seldom a good fit. If you use a triangular slip, take great care to

Fig 4.19 *Using a slip to remove the honing burr and create an inside bevel*

Fig 4.20 *Correct position of gouge and slip if inside bevel is not required*

ensure you do not rub away any of the side wall (Fig 4.21). This also applies when using a knife-edge shaped slipstone. You may find it preferable to remove any burr by cutting with the sharpened V-tool across the end of a piece of coarse wood (Fig 4.22). This method is also effective for taking the burr out of a U-shaped veiner.

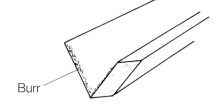

Burr

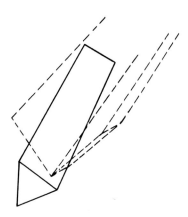

Fig 4.21 *Misfitting or badly aligned triangular slips will cause parts of the blade to wear*

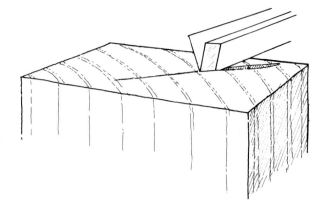

Fig 4.22 *You can remove burr from a V-tool by cutting across the end of a piece of coarse wood*

Stropping

When a tool has been honed it must then be stropped, to produce an even finer cutting edge and to polish the bevel. This helps to burnish each cut you make and to create a reflective surface on the carving. Stropping also restores the cutting edge between honing sessions.

Strops are made from leather with a rough surface, or nap, and you can buy purpose-made ones from craft supply shops. They can be used plain, but better results are achieved if the strop is coated with a polishing agent. Polishing powder mixed to a paste with tallow can be bought ready-prepared from a craft supplier; although chrome polish or any mild abrasive will work, as long as it will stick to the leather. Impregnated strops are also readily available.

The stropping action consists of long strokes pulling the gouge, or chisel, towards you (Fig 4.23). Gouges need to be twisted, so that all the sweep of the cutting edge comes into contact. Only moderate downward pressure is necessary – if you press too hard you may cut the leather.

I like to polish the inside edge of my tools as well as the cutting edge. The easiest way to do this is to make

polishing sticks from pieces of split bamboo cane, shaped to suit the basic gouge sweeps, covered with soft leather and coated with strop paste. Rub the stick inside the blade edge to bring it to a polished surface.

After stropping, test the cutting edge by slicing across the end grain of a piece of pine. If the cut is clean, your tool is sharp; but if the grain shows signs of having been torn, the tool is not sharp enough.

Mechanical honing and stropping

By far the best way is to sharpen mechanically (Fig 4.24). The degree of sharpness will be greater, and it is a lot easier to do. Honing machines all work on the same basic principle: a rotating wheel coated with honing paste trails the tool bevel to produce a razor-sharp cutting edge. Buffing wheels may be included. The machines are so simple to use that you will find little problem keeping your tools in first-class order, but you must follow the manufacturer's instructions carefully.

Two well-known models are illustrated: the English Ashley Iles system (Fig 4.25) and the German Koch machine (Fig 4.26).

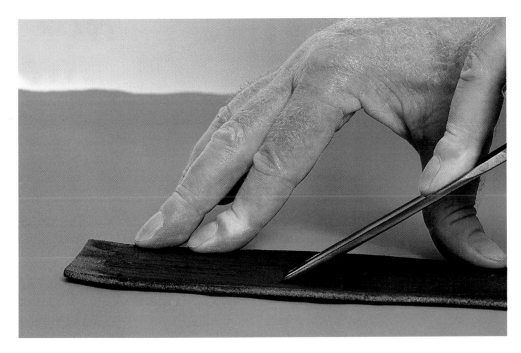

Fig 4.23 *Stropping the cutting edge*

Fig 4.24 *Using an electric honing machine*

Fig 4.25 *The Ashley Iles honing system*

Fig 4.26 *The Kurt Koch honing system. The four wheels are* (left to right) *for sharpening chisels, sharpening gouges, grinding gouges and grinding chisels*

Grinding

Unless you are skilled at using a dry grinding wheel, don't do it. You can ruin a gouge by overheating – this destroys the temper of the steel and turns the blade tip blue. Should a tool be damaged, most repairs are far better done slowly on a coarse-grade oilstone. Remedial work is always best carried out on the sides of the stone.

But if you really must grind, here are a few tips. Firstly, the larger the diameter of the wheel the better – you do not want to hollow-grind the bevel. Secondly, a wet-stone grinder generates far less heat and is less likely to do

any damage than a dry-stone version. For ordinary dry grinders use a 'white' wheel, as they produce less friction. Thirdly, dip the whole blade into cold water after each stroke across the wheel. Lastly, take plenty of time and avoid using excessive pressure. Always wear safety glasses.

A better alternative is to use an inverted belt sander mounted at a 20° incline to give the correct bevel angle, as shown in Fig 4.27. But, again, be sure to take safety precautions, and frequently quench the blade in cold water to prevent the temper of the steel being damaged.

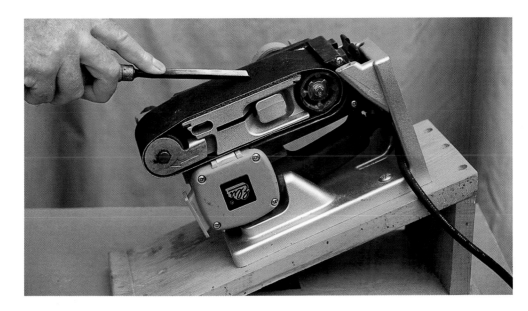

Fig 4.27 *Grinding with a belt sander mounted on a 20° ramp*

Basic sharpening faults

A number of problems can crop up when sharpening your tools. The most common faults relate to the shape of the cutting edge, which should ideally be straight across, at right angles to the blade, or very slightly convex (Fig 4.28). It should be neither too rounded, nor hollow (Fig 4.29). Rounding over is caused by twisting the gouge past the blade corners when honing. Hollowing is due to insufficient rotation during honing. It pays to check blades with a straightedge after honing.

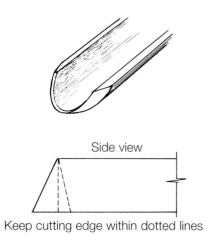

Side view

Keep cutting edge within dotted lines

Fig 4.30 *Avoid extending the nose of the blade*

Blade geometry is important because, when in use, all the sweep should be capable of coming into contact with the wood at more or less the same time to produce a clean cut. If the blade is misshapen, torn wood will result.

Viewed from the side of the blade, the bevel should be perpendicular, or slightly inclined inwards at the bottom (Fig 4.30). If the blade has been sharpened with an extended nose, it will cut badly and tear out the grain, or even cause the wood to split. The only exception is if a V-tool is needed to reach into a confined space, in which case the tip would have to project forwards. Then it is best to have a V-tool specially ground to shape.

Another common fault is when the main bevel becomes too short, or rounded. This normally only applies to the two-bevel method of honing. Every time a tool is sharpened on an oilstone using the two-bevel method, the length of the main bevel is fractionally reduced, until the point is reached when the bevel becomes too short and its angle is too steep to cut properly. To avoid this, once in a while it will be necessary to hone only the back bevel, by placing the gouge on the oilstone with only the main bevel touching. Remedial work is best carried out using firstly a coarse India stone. This problem doesn't occur with the single-bevel sharpening method, since the bevel is extended with each honing operation.

Straight across

Slight radius

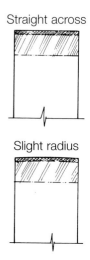

Fig 4.28 *Hone at right angles to the blade, or with a slight radius.*

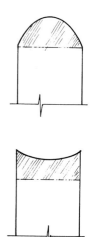

Fig 4.29 *Avoid honing too rounded, or hollow*

If the angle is not kept constant when honing, you will produce a rounded bevel which causes the cutting edge to lift on contact with the wood (Fig 4.31), and gives the impression that the blade is blunt. Avoid handle wobble when using an oilstone. The problem happens less when gouges are mechanically honed.

Curved and spoon-shaped gouges seldom cut well when there is a definite heel at the rear of the bevel (Fig 4.32). Ideally the back of the bevel needs to be blended into the blade. Unfortunately, manufacturers can overlook this when the bevel is originally ground.

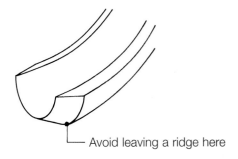

— Avoid leaving a ridge here

Fig 4.32 *A ridge at the back of the bevel will cause a spoon to lift and not cut properly*

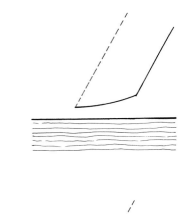

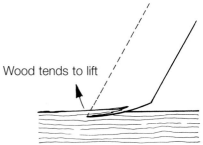

Wood tends to lift

Fig 4.31 *Blade lifting because of a rounded bevel*

Summary

● You will only carve well if your tools are sharp.

● Check the shape of the cutting bevel frequently. Store your gouges so they cannot knock together. Use a tool roll, drawers with individual compartments, or a rack on the workshop wall.

● Don't store carving tools mixed up with rasps, as their cutting edges will get damaged.

● Oilstones and slips should be wiped dry immediately after use, and not left for the oil to dry on them.

5 methods of holding work

It is essential that your work is always securely held in place. Trying to carve a piece of wood which is constantly slipping around is both hazardous and inefficient.

The workbench

The first step is a suitable workbench. An ordinary carpentry bench, or even a strongly made table, will do to start with. If the bench is fitted with an end vice and built-in fixing points such as bench-dogs, so much the better, as they will provide some firm points for holding your wood.

But the ideal position for carving is more upright than for general woodwork, and the trouble with most benches and tables is that they are too low for comfort. Bending over your work can quickly induce severe backache. What is more, most benches are too long for the average size of carved panel or plaque, and can restrict your movement. For these reasons you may eventually wish to construct a separate carving bench, as you cannot buy benches built specifically for the purpose. A worktop measuring about 26 x 25in (660 x 630mm), with a height of between 34 and 36in (860–920mm) depending on your own height, is normally ideal (Fig 5.1).

Securing the wood

The most common method of securing wood is with G-clamps. The only disadvantage can be the height at which the clamp stands above the wood (Fig 5.2). On small work they can get in the way when you are carving. Sometimes a bench holdfast (Fig 5.3) is used, either in conjunction with a G-clamp or alone, for holding the wood in place.

My preference, whenever possible, is to use a backing board held to the bench by G-clamps, with a frame of wooden strips pinned to it in order to hold the carving in place (Figs 5.4 and 5.5). If the strips making up the frame are suitably shaped, oval or circular panels can be held with ease. This arrangement allows the carving to be turned around for ease of working, and the piece can be quickly removed when checking progress. The backing board ensures that the G-clamps are kept well away from the carving, and also helps to protect your bench from accidental damage.

Fig 5.1 *A carving bench*

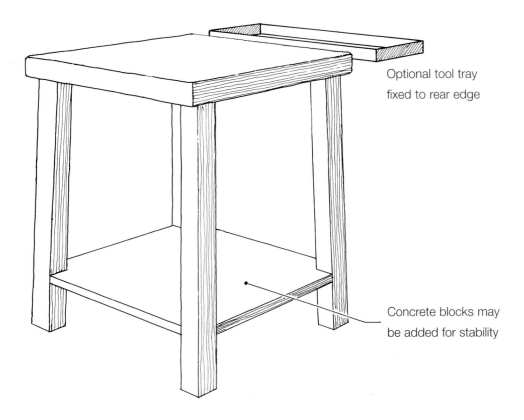

Optional tool tray
fixed to rear edge

Concrete blocks may
be added for stability

Fig 5.2 *Wood secured
with G-clamps*

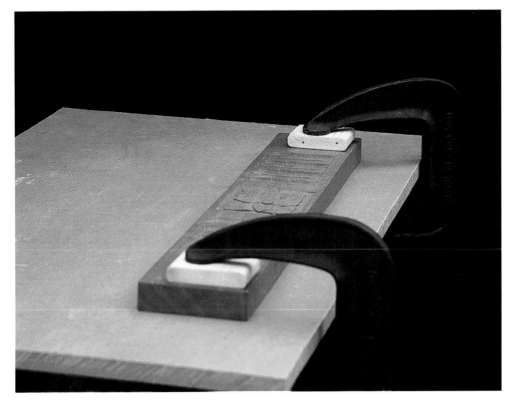

Fig 5.3 *Securing wood with a bench holdfast*

Fig 5.4 *Use a frame of four plywood or hardwood strips to hold your work in place; secure to the workbench by G-clamps*

Fig 5.5 *Backing board and wooden frame ready for use*

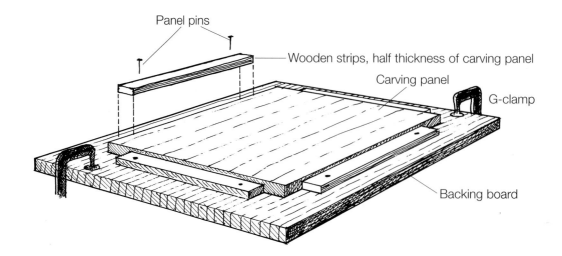

Panel pins

Wooden strips, half thickness of carving panel

Carving panel

G-clamp

Backing board

Fig 5.6 *Using cleats to hold a carving, protecting the work with scrap wood spacers*

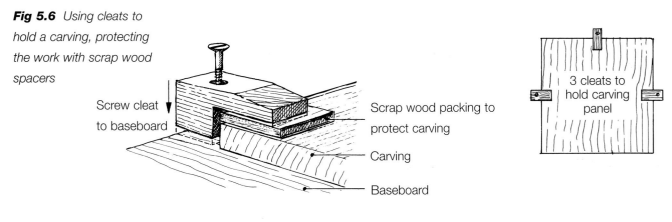

Screw cleat to baseboard

Scrap wood packing to protect carving

Carving

Baseboard

3 cleats to hold carving panel

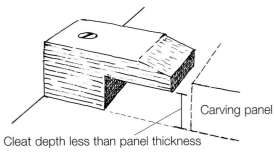

Carving panel

Cleat depth less than panel thickness

Another use of a backing board is when working a very small carving, such as a roundel or other individual motif. In this case the carving wood can be screwed to the backing board from behind; or shallow work can be temporarily glued down.

Some carvers favour the use of small cleats, or blocks, to hold work in place. You will need three cleats to hold one carving, and you must always protect your work with a spacer or scrap of wood set between the cleat and the carving (Fig 5.6). This use of spacers applies equally if you use G-clamps directly on a carving.

Irrespective of how the work is secured, carving is generally carried out with the wood lying flat on the bench to give the greatest support. But if the work involves

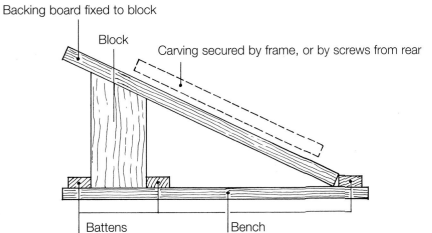

Backing board fixed to block

Block

Carving secured by frame, or by screws from rear

Battens

Bench

Fig 5.7 *Perspective carvings can be raised on blocks and worked on an incline to get better light*

perspective detail, it can be helpful to incline the wood using wedges (Fig 5.7) to take advantage of light cast onto it. An incline of around 25–40° is normally sufficient. Many carvers who do a lot of work of this nature find a swivel-type carving vice helpful for smaller pieces, as it permits the carving to be rotated at will (Fig 5.8). A robust easel is useful for larger panels. Initially, however, you will find it best to have the carving flat on the bench.

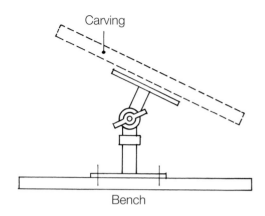

Fig 5.8 *A swivelling vice is useful for viewing your work in perspective*

Summary

- Make sure your working position is really comfortable, and adjust the bench height if necessary.

- Consider using a backing board to hold your work, which facilitates ease of working and protects the surface of your bench.

- Use G-clamps to hold your work initially, then try other methods of work-holding as your skill develops.

- Work with the carving flat on the bench, unless you are carving perspective detail.

6 basic cuts

Even if you are already experienced in other forms of woodwork, you will probably find it useful to practise some basic cuts before you start work on an actual carving.

How to hold a gouge or chisel

Holding the gouge correctly is essential both for good workmanship and for safety. There are two methods you need to know: holding a tool when using a mallet, and when using hand pressure alone.

Fig 6.1 shows how a gouge is held when using a mallet. To prevent the gouge slipping, the little finger can be wrapped around the base of the handle. Keep your thumb down, in contact with the index finger; don't let it stick upwards.

Fig 6.2 shows how a gouge or chisel is held right-handedly when it is being used with hand pressure only. Note the position of the fingers holding the blade – this provides counter-pressure to control the forward force of the cut. Also note how the heel of the left hand holding the blade rests on the wood, giving stability and assisting accurate cutting.

At no time should any part of the hand be in front of the blade, as shown in Fig 6.3. Make sure you always cut away from yourself, and never towards your body.

Cutting with a V-tool

The V-tool is a versatile instrument which can be used as a pencil for 'drawing' shapes on the wood. It is also used for incising lines to mark out a relief design prior to background removal, making a straightforward V-shaped channel outside the main design (Fig 6.4).

Another use of the V-tool is to cut decorative patterns, which are often used as component parts of designs on furniture. When cutting an incised pattern the V-tool can be twisted over to produce a slanting cut, so more light will fall on one side of the cut than the other (Fig 6.5). How much the tool is tilted will depend on how much emphasis you require. When cutting an S-bend, as in Fig 6.5, you can maintain the same twist around both curves or reverse the angle of the twist, depending on the effect you want

Fig 6.1 *Holding a tool when using a mallet*

Fig 6.2 *Holding a tool when carving with hand pressure alone*

Fig 6.3 **Do not** *cut like this, with any part of the hand in front of the blade*

to achieve. The width of the cut can be adjusted by the amount of downward pressure applied to the tool, so just one V-tool can be used to produce cuts of varying widths.

Never use the V-tool with excessive force. Its side walls are fragile, and can easily be snapped if you dig in too deeply. Try making some straight cuts, followed by a few curved ones.

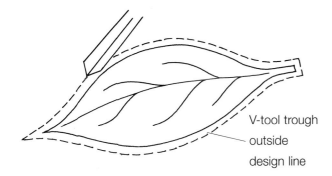

V-tool trough
outside
design line

Fig 6.4 *Using a V-tool to outline a relief design prior to removing the waste wood of the background*

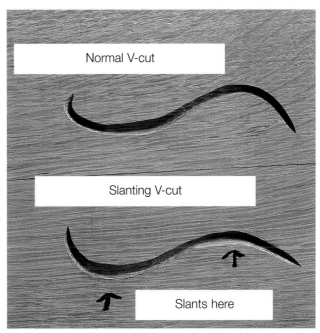

Normal V-cut

Slanting V-cut

Slants here

Fig 6.5 *V-tools can be held straight to produce a uniform channel, or twisted over to create an angled cut which allows more light to fall on one side of the channel*

Cutting with a no. 11 veiner

The veiner is also used for making decorative lines, and like the V-tool it can be used for marking out patterns. But unlike the V-tool, which produces a visually hard line, the look of the veiner's cut is less obtrusive as light does not reflect off the sides of the groove so much (Fig 6.6).

Generally the veiner is used to cut a U-shaped groove; it is seldom if ever tilted. There are, though, times when it can usefully be employed to sever small areas of waste wood within a design. Try some shallow cuts, and compare them with those you made with the V-tool.

Cutting with a gouge

With all your gouges, start by using short strokes. This will help you to work to a uniform depth of cut (Fig 6.7). As your cutting action becomes more fluid, your strokes will lengthen naturally.

When removing waste wood, it is better to cut either diagonally or at right angles to the line of the grain (Fig 6.8), which minimizes the chance of the wood splitting. Only when you have gained some experience is it safe to take liberties by purposely splitting off the wood in a controlled manner.

When cutting up to an edge, make the last cuts *inwards* from the edge, back towards the main part of the wood, and not from the edge out into space (Fig 6.9). Cutting inwards ensures support for the stroke, which will produce a clean cut. If you do it the other way round there will be no support for the last part of the cut and the wood will break off.

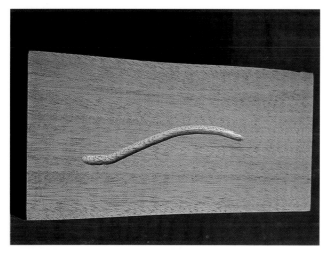

Fig 6.6 *Cut created with a no. 11 veiner*

Fig 6.7 *Use short strokes initially to obtain a uniform depth of cut*

Fig 6.8 Remove waste wood by cutting diagonally or at right angles to the direction of the grain

Fig 6.9 Cut inwards from an edge to support your stroke

Depth of cut

A gouge only works as a cutting instrument when the sharp edge of the blade is in contact with the wood. If you cut too deeply, the top edges of the sides of the gouge blade act like wedges, causing the wood to be split apart rather than cleanly cut. It is therefore essential always to work within the depth of cut permitted by the sweep of the gouge (Figs 6.10 and 6.11). This is why such a range of tools is made.

Try to avoid using the flatter gouges, such as nos. 3 or 4, when there is much wood to remove; they will only leave a ragged cut. It is best to start with a gouge with a

Fig 6.10 Cut well within the depth of the gouge sweep to avoid splitting the wood

steeper sweep, such as no. 5 or no. 9, then progress to the flatter ones. No. 9 is a quick-cut gouge; its sweep allows deep cuts to be made, which speedily remove excess wood. Think in terms of only ever cutting to a depth of half or two-thirds of the sweep, and you will always make clean cuts.

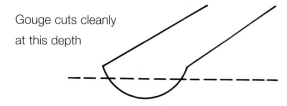

Gouge cuts cleanly at this depth

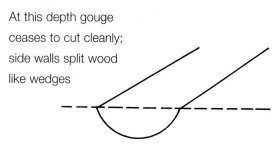

At this depth gouge ceases to cut cleanly; side walls split wood like wedges

Fig 6.11 Correct and incorrect cutting depths

Cutting with the lie of the grain

If you make some shallow test cuts you will find that in one direction you will produce bright and shiny cuts; this is when you are cutting with the lie of the grain. If you reverse the direction your cuts will be dull and slightly rough, because you are cutting against the grain. Wherever possible – and it will not always be so – try and cut with the grain (Fig 6.12).

Stab-cuts

At various times you will need to make downward stab-cuts into the wood. It will happen initially when you are setting in the basic design and removing the surrounding waste wood, and later on when you model the design.

Fig 6.13 shows a gouge or chisel entering the wood to make a stab-cut. The wood is compressed by the blade thickness, and when the blade pressure is released the damaged fibres will fracture. The weakness caused in this way can result in the wood fracturing when you do the final modelling. But if you cut back progressively to the final line of the design you will avoid this problem, as the

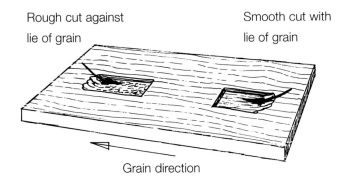

Rough cut against lie of grain

Smooth cut with lie of grain

Grain direction

Fig 6.12 *Cutting with the lie of the grain*

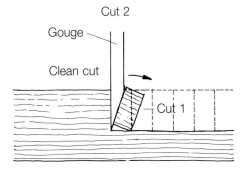

Cut 2

Gouge

Clean cut

Cut 1

On cut 2, pressure is towards the weaker area adjacent to cut 1

Fig 6.14 *Stab-cutting in from an edge to prevent the wood fracturing*

blade pressure is then directed towards the waste area (Fig 6.14).

Stab-cutting in line with the grain will cause the wood to split on either side of the tool, due to the wedging action of the blade (Fig 6.15). To prevent this, make a stop-cut across the grain before making the in-line cut.

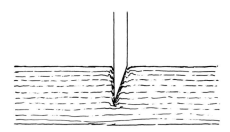

When blade enters wood, surrounding cells and fibres are compressed

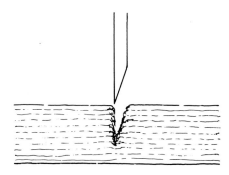

When pressure is released, cells and fibres will fracture

Fig 6.13 *The effect of stab-cuts on wood*

Splits occur here when tool is used in line with the grain

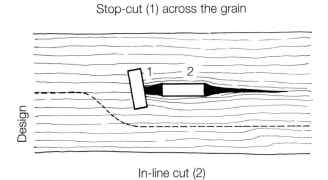

Stop-cut (1) across the grain

Design

In-line cut (2)

Fig 6.15 *Wood splits when stab-cut in line with the grain. Make a stop-cut across the grain to prevent splitting*

Using a spoon gouge

While it is unlikely that you will need to use a spoon gouge for the first carvings you do, it may still be worthwhile knowing at this stage how the cutting action is performed.

A spoon gouge is designed to take deep cuts when hollows are being carved. Beyond a certain depth ordinary straight gouges are ineffective, but the cranked shape of the spoon enables it to work in a recess or hollow without difficulty.

The action needed to cut with a spoon is not so much a matter of pushing the gouge forwards, as is the case with the straight-bladed types, but manipulating the handle through a downward arc while exerting slight forward pressure (Fig 6.16). If the handle moves in an arc, the cutting edge will move in the opposite direction – as

the handle drops, the tip of the blade lifts. When cutting with a spoon gouge, it is important to think of what is happening to the handle, while observing the movement of the blade tip. It can be useful to add a twisting action as the cut takes place, which will help to sever the wood fibres.

While there is still a lot more to learn about using carving tools, you will certainly find it useful to try out the various cuts I have described before you tackle your first carving project. Use an easily worked, close-grained wood, such as lime, if you can.

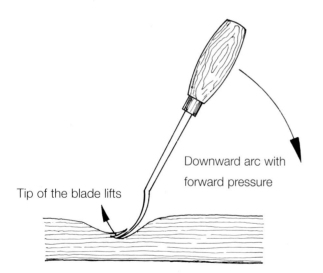

Downward arc with forward pressure

Tip of the blade lifts

Fig 6.16 *Handle and blade action when cutting with a spoon gouge*

Summary

- Always hold the tools safely.

- The V-tool can be used for 'drawing' on the wood.

- Cut diagonally across the grain, if you can, when removing waste wood.

- Cut in from an edge.

- Take shallow cuts – don't bury the gouge.

- Cut with the lie of the grain wherever possible.

- Stab-cut across the grain prior to cutting with it.

7 design and drawing

Design considerations

As discussed in the Introduction to this book, low relief is the most popular form of decorative carving. All repetitive designs – patterns which repeat at regular intervals, such as along a frieze – are generally better suited to a shallow treatment and are carved in low relief.

Solitary features requiring emphasis are more effective when worked deeply in high relief, which sometimes verges on three-dimensional sculpture. High-relief work can be exciting, but time-consuming. Initially I suggest you concentrate on low relief.

The treatment of plaques, panels or mirrors will vary depending on the subject. There is no arbitrary figure of depth which indicates that the treatment is specifically one form or the other. Sometimes a design may call for both low and high relief: some parts of a plaque, for example, will be carved to stand out from the background, while other parts will be kept shallow. In fact, the more variation a carving has in its feature levels, the more interesting it will be.

As a general rule, though, any part of a design which incorporates delicate detail has to be kept close to the background, simply because it would otherwise become too fragile. Think of the long-term durability of the carving. A deeply cut piece of work as delicate as gossamer might be a fine exercise in skilful carving, but one could question its practical use.

Start by planning to work within a depth of no more than about ½in (10mm or so). This will give you scope to develop depth levels and the flexibility to correct mistakes. It is far more taxing to produce a good shallow carving than one of moderate depth.

Beginners may wonder how to treat overlapping parts of a design in order to retain a realistic look, yet still keep to a shallow depth. But design elements which overlap one another, such as branches or stems, tend to look odd when each part is carved to its full depth. You can obtain a more realistic look if at the point of intersection the two parts are carved to only half their normal depth. Show that the minor branch passes beneath by dipping it to half the depth of the major branch where they meet (Figs 7.1 and 7.2).

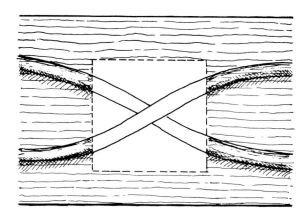

Fig 7.1 *Overlapping design elements can cause problems at their point of intersection*

The project examples in this book have been chosen to build up your skill, but sooner or later you will want to create original designs of your own . So let us now look at some of the aspects of making designs, and how to prepare drawings.

Planning the drawing

It is vital to plan drawings with some regard to the smallest size of tool you have. It is so easy to design a piece of work incorporating, for example, narrow gaps between foliage, then find you just don't have a gouge small enough to make the cuts. If, for example, your narrowest gouge is the 1⁄16in (1.5mm) no. 11 veiner, then the smallest space between parts of the carving will need to be wider than this to facilitate ease of working. There should be enough space to allow the tool to enter the gap comfortably. One way of ensuring this is to do the final drawing using a felt-tip pen rather than a pencil, as it gives a thicker line allowing more leeway when actually carving; conté-crayons and charcoal sticks also work well.

Avoid making your drawings too complicated. Too much detail can be confusing when transferred on to the wood. It helps to think along the lines of a picture painted in oils with broad strokes, rather than a watercolour. This does not mean to say you will never produce finely

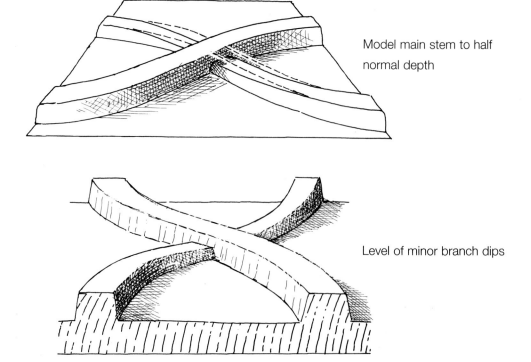

Model main stem to half normal depth

Level of minor branch dips

Fig 7.2 *Model overlapping design elements to only half their normal depth to create a realistic intersection*

carved, delicate work – simply that it will take patience and a lot of practice.

Matching the design to the wood

It helps if you can relate the design you have in mind to the type of timber you plan to use. This will overcome the problem of trying to carve a subject in a wood totally unsuited for the purpose. Basically, if the carving is of a delicate nature, you will need a close-grained, easily worked wood with an unobtrusive grain. If the carving is more robust, the wood can afford to be coarser and the grain stronger.

In the case of furniture carving there is usually little or no option as to the type of wood. Then it is a case of making quite sure you are not tempted to use a treatment unsuitable for the wood. For example, fine and delicate carving is seldom carried out in oak. Delicacy has its place, if only to show the carver's skill, but there are times when over-refinement can be a mistake.

In the case of wall plaques, or whenever dimensions are critical, you will find it pays to select the piece of wood first, then do the design. Taking things in that order you never should run out of wood. Do the design first, and you may experience problems fitting the drawing to the timber.

Viewing distance

When planning the design, think where the carving will be placed and from how far away it will be viewed. In architectural work the distance may be considerable, and the structure of the carving will need to take this into account. A ceiling boss in a church would require bold carving to be seen from ground level. But a plaque could be more delicately carved with greater detail and finesse, as its viewing distance may be only a matter of a few feet (a metre or two). The same applies to most furniture work.

Drawing

Build up a portfolio of ideas. Take photographs of flowers in bloom – one day you may need to carve a particular flower out of season. Both colour slides and prints are useful. You can scale up better by projecting slides onto white card and drawing around the image.

Remember that if you work from magazine or book illustrations they will usually carry a copyright restriction. By all means use them to stimulate your own ideas, but try to be original.

Unless there is a definite reason for using a rectilinear structure, a drawing should be composed of a series of flowing lines. (However, if you do need to produce mathematically accurate designs, the Appendix on pages 140–5 gives information on geometric drawing.) If you look at nature you will find that most natural shapes flow and curve; seldom is there any angular make-up. Look at how leaves join to a stem – each intersection has a small radius. A flower stem will look more attractive drawn with a slight curve than perpendicularly. Flowing lines can also work in sympathy with the grain, or figuring, of the wood, giving emphasis to your work.

A good tip is to use French curves, obtainable from most art supply shops. They normally come in a set of three, and offer a wide variety of curves and scrolls. With these you should have little difficulty in creating flowing designs.

● **Equal-sided designs** Should you wish to use a design where one side is a mirror image of the other, you only need to draw one half; simply turning over the paper will give you an identical design in reverse for the other half (Fig 7.3).

● **Paper** Layout paper is ideal for drawing designs, and less costly than tracing paper. It is thin enough to allow you to superimpose two or more sheets without loss of detail, which helps considerably when building up a pattern. Just start a few sheets down into the pad, and mark in the area of the wood with a broad black line. You will be able to see this through any subsequent sheets which may be needed while you finalize the design.

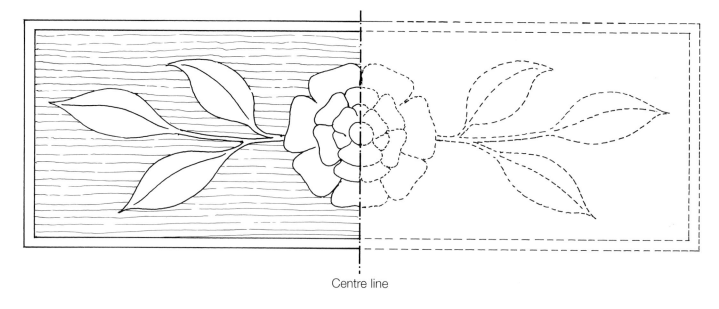

Centre line

Fig 7.3 *Producing a mirror image design by reversing the paper*

Layout paper is available in standard-size pads, of which A3 (16½ x 11¾in/420 x 297mm) and A4 (11¾ x 8¼in/297 x 210mm) are the most useful. You will find it better to work with layout paper than normal-weight drawing paper, but squared graph paper may be used instead.

Other aids to drawing are a clear plastic ruler, a compass, a protractor, and both 45° and 60° set squares. Good drawing pencils and charcoal or conté-crayons are essential. I prefer to use pencil grades B and 2B, which are moderately soft. You will also need a selection of felt pens and a pack of mixed coloured chalks.

Sectional sketches

Relief carvings seldom have a flat surface; ideally they should always contain contour features to reflect light. This means there will be low areas as well as high spots. To create these you must understand the three-dimensional make-up of the design.

For example, consider the true shape of a simple flower. In plan form (Fig 7.4) you see the basic elements, such as the petals leading out from the calyx, the stem, and perhaps some leaves.

What you do not see, though, is how each part relates to the other in respect of contour – how, for instance, the petals curve and bend; how the stem leads to the back of the flower-head. You can apply a little shading, as shown, to indicate low areas, but this does not tell you how deep these low areas really are. So you need to make additional

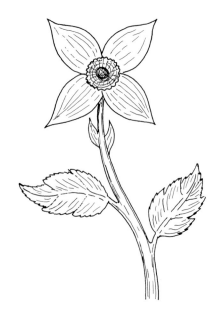

Fig 7.4 *Flat plan drawing of flower*

Fig 7.5 Sectional
sketches through parts of
the flower

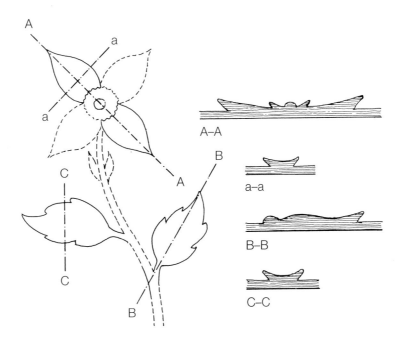

sketches detailing sections through various parts of the
design to tell you what the shapes are like in contour and
in depth (Fig 7.5).

In addition to the sectional shapes you will need to
consider the overall contour effect of the carving. All relief
work has to be made up of a series of levels. There will be
high points, areas of mid-level, and low parts of the carving
falling close to the background. It is the arrangement of
these levels which will give interest to your work. The
degree of variation is dependent only upon the total depth
of wood available and whether you are working in low or
high relief. For example, if you examine the relief design on
a coin you will see how shallow it can be, yet still retain
some contour effect.

To plot these main levels you may find it helpful to use
coloured chalk. You could use red for the high parts,
brown for mid-range areas, and green for the low-lying
parts of the design. All you then need to do is shade the
various parts of the drawing according to how you
perceive its depth – in effect making a colour contour map
(Fig 7.6). Once the drawing has been transferred to the
wood you can repeat the colouring on the wood itself.

Low level	Mid-level	High level

Fig 7.6 Colour coding can be added to plan view of
flower to identify contours

When planning the drawing, you need to ensure that the primary elements follow the grain pattern of the wood you propose to use. It is usual for the grain to run along the design (Fig 7.7). It is also essential for delicate parts which will stand out from the background, such as leaf tips, to follow the line of the grain rather than be placed across it – when they run with the grain they will have more strength and be less prone to break off. If a leaf tip

or similar delicate point does fall on cross grain, keep the carving low to the background (Fig 7.8).

Using a clay model

Unless you are well acquainted with the subject, or have a well-developed sense of three-dimensional visualization, you may find you get a mental block when trying to work out a subject's contour shape. Making a clay model, technically known as a **maquette**, will help in these instances (Fig 7.9).

You can use either a synthetic modelling material, such as Plasticine, or ordinary potter's clay for these models; I prefer to work in clay, which is inexpensive to buy. In either case, knead your material well before use, so it becomes easily workable. You will need very little equipment to make your clay model: just your fingers, a spatula for shaping, a small blade for cutting, a paintbrush, and a sponge and water.

Copying designs onto wood

Carbon paper is generally used to transfer the design to the wood, and is available in several different types.

Blue carbon paper is pencil grade, and shows up well when imprinted onto the wood. However, being soft, it can smudge, and it is difficult to remove surplus carbon from the wood. **Black** carbon paper – typewriter grade –

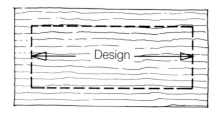

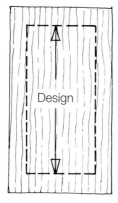

Fig 7.7 *Plan the main design element to run with the grain*

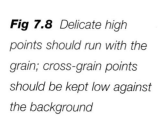

Fig 7.8 *Delicate high points should run with the grain; cross-grain points should be kept low against the background*

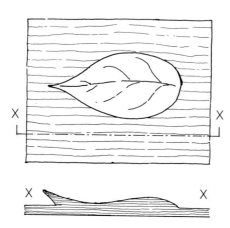

Tip can be high if running with the grain

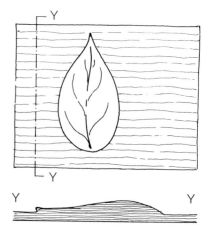

On cross grain, keep tip low

Fig 7.9 Use a clay model
to help work out contour
shapes

needs more imprint pressure, which can leave marks on
the surface of the wood.

Erasable carbon paper (one make is Transtrace) can
be bought from specialist graphic design shops. It leaves
a graphite imprint on the wood which is easily removed
with a pencil eraser. Though more expensive than ordinary
carbon paper, erasable paper is more convenient to use.

Drawings can be held onto the wood with either
masking tape or Blu-Tack on two corners. Slide the
carbon paper underneath the drawing and trace over your
design using a coloured ballpoint pen. The difference in
colour will help to avoid missing out parts of the design
when you imprint through the carbon paper.

Summary

● Draw the main part of the design with broad
  lines.

● Use layout paper.

● Draw with flowing curves wherever possible.

● Make sectional sketches.

● Think of the contours.

● Match the wood to the design.

● Work with the run of the grain.

your first carvings

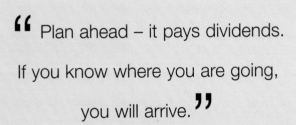

" Plan ahead – it pays dividends.

If you know where you are going,

you will arrive. "

8 carving in low relief

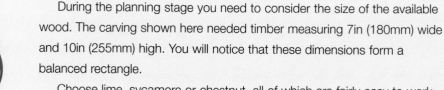
Project: Carving a flower

Let's start carving! As this is your first attempt, plan to use a design of a reasonable size, which is simpler to carve.

During the planning stage you need to consider the size of the available wood. The carving shown here needed timber measuring 7in (180mm) wide and 10in (255mm) high. You will notice that these dimensions form a balanced rectangle.

Choose lime, sycamore or chestnut, all of which are fairly easy to work. I used quarter-sawn lime, 1in (25mm) thick, which was then planed on both sides to give a smooth surface.

Drawing the design

Start by making a drawing on layout paper of the design you wish to carve (Fig 8.1). Select the diameters of the circles required for the flower with reference to the sizes of the tools you will be using. This carving was carried out with those listed as a basic selection in Chapter 3 (page 33). If the flower is too small it may prove difficult to carve, as your tools will be too big to make the necessary fine cuts. I made the diameter of the centre circle ¾in (20mm), and the outer one 2¾in (70mm).

It may prove useful to fix the petal positions by using a protractor to mark out the angles. Divide 360° by the number of petals to be drawn. In this example there are five petals, so their position at the midpoint of each one will be 72°. Then draw in their shapes freehand, using the outer circle (shown as a dotted line in Fig 8.1) as a guide. Some of the petal edges may fall outside the outer circle and some within it, depending on how they are designed.

Draw in the centre line of the stem, making sure it lines up with the centre of the circles. Use a flowing curve. Then draw in the sides of the stem to produce a gentle taper up to the flower.

When you draw the leaves, make sure there is sufficient gap between them and the stem. The gap needs to be about 50% greater than the width of the tool you propose to use in cutting. I planned to cut this area with the ¼in (6mm) no. 9 gouge.

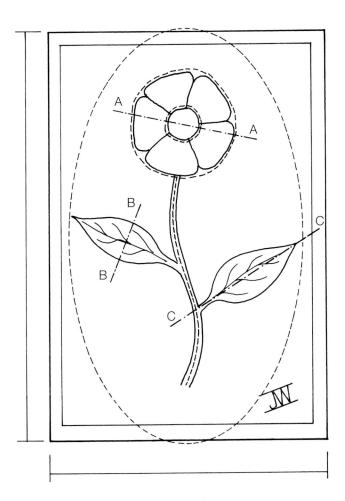

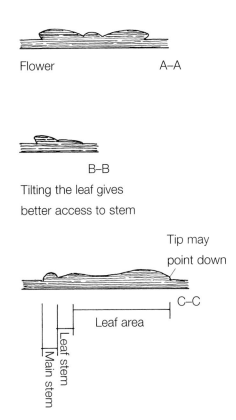

Flower   A–A

B–B

Tilting the leaf gives
better access to stem

Tip may
point down

C–C

Leaf area

Leaf stem

Main stem

Fig 8.1 *Flat plan drawing of the flower carving,
and sectional sketches across the contours*

When you have completed the drawing, make sectional
sketches as shown in Fig 8.1. Plot the high and low parts
of the design, including how the petals overlap, by using
coloured chalks on your plan drawing – you could use red
for high points, brown for mid-range areas, and green for
low-lying parts. This will give you, in effect, a contour map
to guide you when you carve. Build up your mental picture
of the finished work. It is just like starting a journey: if you
know where you are going, and you have a map, you will
arrive. If you set off without either, you will probably get
lost. Plan ahead – it pays dividends. If you wish to include
a personal monogram, put it in now.

Consider the shape of the background and the style of
border it will have. I opted for a rectangle with a bevelled,

or chamfered, edge (Fig 8.2). Note that it is easier to work
the background to a level surface if you do not have a
raised border.

An oval-shaped panel would need a symmetrical
outline, which is easy to produce. When you have
completed the drawing of the flower, simply fold the paper
in four, as shown, and trim the loose edges to a chosen

Raised   Bevelled

Fig 8.2 *Choose either a raised or a bevelled edge*

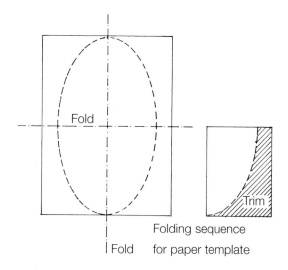

Folding sequence
for paper template

Fig 8.3 *Creating an oval border*

curve (Fig 8.3). When you open out the sheet the curve
will carry right around the outer edge. See page 142 for
more on this.

Planning the carving depth

Plan to carve to a maximum depth of around ½in (about
10mm) and mark the edges of the board accordingly.
Slightly above this line, mark in a dotted line as a safety
net (Fig 8.4). Initially, all the cutting out of waste wood
(roughing out) and setting in of the design is done to

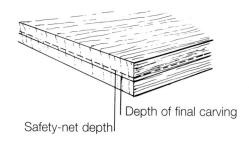

Depth of final carving
Safety-net depth

Fig 8.4 *Marking the safety-net depth*

the depth of the dotted line. This will ensure that you are
not left with unsightly cut marks in the final background
(Fig 8.5).

You may feel that the depth mentioned is quite deep
for a low-relief carving. It has been chosen on purpose,
since it will give you ample latitude to create all the
contours you need. Working to a tight, or close, tolerance
is fine when you have developed your carving skill, but it
does leave little or no margin for error. A very low relief is
more difficult to work than a deeper carving.

Outlining the design

Apply the design to the wood using carbon paper, tracing
over the drawing with a ballpoint pen. You may find it
useful to go over the outline on the wood afterwards with

Fig 8.5 *Depth line marked
on the sides of the wood
(continuous line). Dotted
lines both on the sides and
around the design act as a
safety net*

Fig 8.6 *Incising the outline of the design*

a felt-tip pen to give a bolder outline. Then stand back and take a good look, to see if you wish to make any changes to the design. Now is the time to do it.

Use the V-tool to cut a trench around the outside of the design (Fig 8.6). Do this by lining up one corner of the blade on the drawing. The cut of the V will then be just out in the waste wood. Small areas of detail can be ignored at this stage by skipping round them. Cutting the trench in the waste wood gives you a second safety net, and allows you to remove all the surplus background without damaging the design. Whether or not you use a mallet for this work will depend largely on the type of wood you are using: you can cut the trench using simply hand pressure if the wood is soft enough, but most carvers prefer to use a mallet for greater accuracy.

Groundwork

In this project all the background is removed to a uniform level. Sometimes, though, relief carvings can have a dished or saucer-shaped background; or the design may be just recessed into a flat surface (a useful technique for furniture which must be comfortable to sit on). As your skill develops you can experiment with different types of background treatment.

Start removing the waste wood with the ¼in (6mm) no. 9 gouge. Use a mallet or, if you prefer, just hand

pressure (excessive mallet force can cause stress to the surrounding wood). Work inwards away from the outer edges, keeping the depth of cut even, and cut either diagonally or at right angles to the grain (Fig 8.7). Do not cut so deeply that you wedge out the wood. To avoid cutting into the design, make sure you end the cuts just short of the V-tool trench.

As the background becomes deeper, switch over to using a flatter gouge like the no. 6, followed by the no. 4 or no. 3. This will help to ensure that you avoid cutting through the safety net too soon. When you are making the cuts, be conscious of the distinctive texture effect which each gouge produces. This can provide valuable experience when you come to decide the final treatment of the background.

Getting to the point of carving the actual design can be a lengthy business if much background wood has to be removed first. It is possible to speed up the process by mechanical means. A router, if you have one, will quickly remove the waste wood, but be sure that you only cut as deep as the *dotted* depth line. This will enable you to finish off with gouge cuts in order to give a natural look to the carving. In many ways, though, it is better to do it all by hand to start with – you will gain so much more experience this way.

Fig 8.7 *Cutting out the waste wood from the background*

Trimming back to the design

When the background wood has been removed down to the safety net, the next step is to trim back to the design itself. Before you start, work out the cutting sequence to ensure you trim with cross-grain stop cuts before cutting with the grain. If you fail to do this you may well split some of the design.

Use vertical cuts back to the V-tool trench, but do not try to remove too much wood with each stroke. Keep outside the design line to begin with. If the gouge bevel is facing away from the design, hold the tool vertically (Fig 8.8); if it is towards the design, angle the tool outwards, so that the bevel cuts down vertically (Fig 8.9). Your gouges must be razor-sharp, as much of the cutting will be on end grain and the wood needs to be cut cleanly. The depth to which you cut is important, and you must carefully gauge the amount of downward pressure you apply. If it is too little you will fail to carry the cut sufficiently deep; too much, and you will leave stab marks in the final background surface.

Concave curves, such as those on the upper edges of the leaves, can be trimmed with the no. 4 gouge. Alternatively, make a number of small cuts using a gouge

Fig 8.8 *Vertical stab-cuts with the gouge bevel facing away from the design*

Fig 8.9 *When the gouge bevel faces towards the design, hold the tool at an angle to make vertical stab-cuts*

with a steeper sweep than the shape of the curve. Extended convex curves, like the lower edges of the leaves, can be trimmed by making multiple cuts with the no. 2 skew chisel, or with a shallow-sweep gouge.

Make a few trimming cuts, then remove some of the waste background. Each stabbing cut to trim the design and each paring cut to remove background waste have to meet cleanly: don't break away any of the wood. Work progressively from one to the other. It is not at all unusual for the background to rise up around the design area. Do be aware of this early on, and remove the excess. If you don't, you will certainly have to do it later, which can be troublesome as you will have to re-trim the design.

Keep your options open

No matter how good the original artwork, you sometimes find the need to make slight modifications to the design once the carving gets under way. You may hit on an attractive area of figuring in the wood, which can be used to advantage by altering the design somewhat, or it may just be a case of correcting a mistake. For whatever reason, if you contrive to keep your options going as long as you can, you will retain flexibility of working.

This does not mean that you should be over-cautious or indecisive – good carving requires positive thought and decisive action. But, equally, it does not mean you have to follow blindly what has been drawn, unless of course you are carrying out restoration work or pattern-making. You, as the carver, must have the last word on how the work is to evolve.

To keep your options open, you may not always want to cut to the drawn design immediately just because it is there. In this project I kept an option going regarding the flower stem by initially making it wide. I was then able to form the shape as the carving evolved. I might not have been quite so happy about the design if early on I had locked it into tight parameters by excessive cutting. Having wood to spare can sometimes be just as useful as having money in the bank.

Another worthwhile point to remember is to let the sweeps of your gouges dictate the curves or flutes of the designs you carve. In the early stages of your carving career, when you are acquiring the ability to cut skilfully and learning the characteristics of different woods, it is very helpful to exercise a generous amount of personal interpretation. It is for this very reason that the design of this project is an imaginary flower and not a specific one.

Modelling the design

Modelling the design is the exciting part, when your creative skill can be given full rein. At this point you may well wonder if you have ever really looked, in detail, at a flower or a leaf. And this is just the time to go and do so, before you start. If you can, study the shape of a leaf and a flower similar to the imaginary project design. Examine its contours; see how it curls or twists. If you use your eyes, and remember what you see, your carving will be that much better.

● **Working from low areas to high** I have always found that if you start carving in the high points first, and then work through to the lower levels, the carving invariably ends up deeper than intended. So I do it the other way round instead, fixing the low areas first (as far as the design allows), and only then working up to the high spots.

On this project I therefore made the first modelling cut at the top of the stem, just away from the lowest petal, using the ¼in (6mm) no. 3 gouge (Fig 8.10). I angled the top part of the stem on a steep gradient to a low point at the base of the petal, to suggest how the stem passes to the back of the flower.

Fig 8.10 *Start modelling at a low point in the final carving*

Having established the lowest point of the stem, I fixed the dominant angle of the leaves, slanting their surfaces towards the stem using the ⅝in (15mm) no. 3 gouge this time to make broad cuts. This gave a reasonably flat surface prior to modelling the leaves, and reduced the amount of wood on the inner edges of the leaves to give better access to the adjacent stem.

The position and level of the leaf stems, joining the main stem, was then cut. For this I used the ¼in (6mm) no. 9 gouge, which allowed the leaf stems to dip down from the higher levels of the leaves themselves. Using gouges with steeper sweeps for setting contour levels can be more effective than just using the shallow-cut types, since only a small area of wood can be worked with each stroke. If flatter gouges are used all the time, the chances are that insufficient contour undulation will be developed.

Whether you work the leaves in detail next, or go to the centre of the flower and the lower part of the petals, is a matter of personal choice.

● **The flower centre** The flower centre is a dome, with the highest part being the original wood surface. Around this is a deep depression to show that the petals emanate

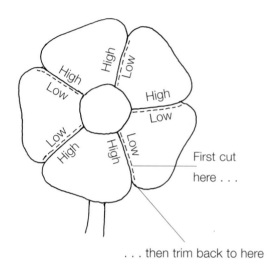

Fig 8.11 *The contours of the petals*

from a lower level. The petals overlap, and have to be set on two levels (Fig 8.11).

Cutting the inner dome requires preliminary stab-cuts to be made outside the circle, so the dome is not subjected to any stress as the gouge enters the wood. Use the ⅜in (9mm) no. 5 (Fig 8.12). The petals are stab-cut in a similar way, using the ⅜in (9mm) no. 4 gouge in

Fig 8.12 *Stab-cutting around the central dome of the flower*

both cases. Use the ½in (12mm) no. 6 to cut the petal trench around the central dome and to delineate the petal contours (Fig 8.13).

For rounding the dome I used two tools: the small ¼in (6mm) no. 3 gouge, inverted, for the initial modelling (Fig 8.14), followed by the skew chisel to perfect the shape (Fig 8.15). You will need to make a slicing cut with the tip of the skew, while rotating the blade to ensure the cutting edge remains correctly aligned to both the shape of the dome and the lie of the grain.

● **Advancing the modelling** Continue carving the flower with light paring cuts with the no. 5 gouge to give each petal a faceted surface. (There is more about texture cutting in the next chapter.) Keep the bevel rubbing on the wood and only raise the tool handle slightly. This will produce cuts of minimal thickness, and prevent the blade from digging in.

Fig 8.14 Preliminary modelling of the central dome

Fig 8.13 Carving the petals

Fig 8.15 Finishing the dome with a skew chisel

Shape the stem with the small no. 3 gouge, or use the skew chisel, and work up to the centre line. Be sure there is an even taper to the stem (Figs 8.16 and 8.17).

Throughout the modelling stage it is vital to cut sympathetically with the wood. You will remember from Chapter 6 (pages 62–3) that if you cut with the lie of the grain you will get a shiny cut, and a rough surface to the cut if you work against the lie of the grain.

At this point in the carving you must also be very much aware of the true nature of your particular piece of wood, and especially how well the cells are bonded together. You can only ever model the design within the capability of the wood. If you want really delicate or intricate detail, you have to be sure the wood is capable of its execution. This project was carved in good-quality lime, which was capable of taking fine detail without fear of bits snapping off. Had it been carved in a coarser type of wood – mahogany, for example – I would certainly have expected

Fig 8.16 *Shaping the stem with the small no. 3 gouge*

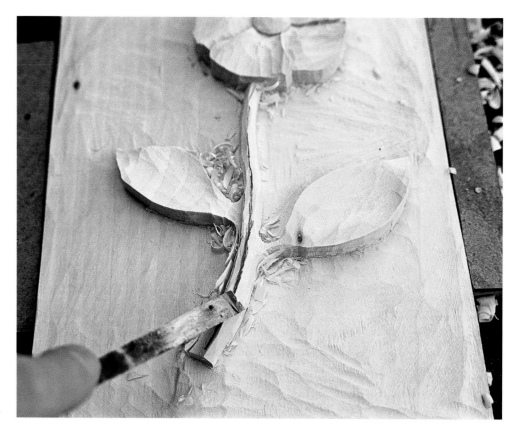

Fig 8.17 *Approaching the centre line with the skew chisel*

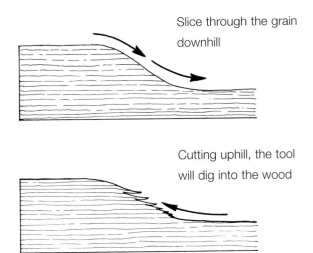

Slice through the grain downhill

Cutting uphill, the tool will dig into the wood

Fig 8.18 *Cut downhill rather than uphill, to avoid digging into the wood*

possible fractures in thin cross-grain parts of the design. But even the best of woods can fracture if the cutting technique is incorrect. One common fault is to try and cut 'uphill', ignoring the fact that the gouge will jab into the various layers of the wood (Fig 8.18).

● **Preventing splits** When stab-cutting and trimming a shape which is in line with the direction of the grain, remember that the wood will split on either side of the tool. In Fig 8.19 the wood could split if you cut first at point A; but if you follow the sequence a to e and use the sweeps shown, there is little chance of splits. Using

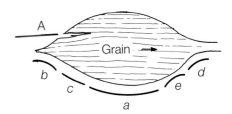

Fig 8.19 *Cutting with the lie of the grain (A) will cause splits – follow the sequence a–e to avoid this*

shallow sweeps facing the curve helps to shape a convex curve, but it is easier to cut a concave with a steep sweep facing outwards. And don't lever out the wood instead of cutting it cleanly away.

As you model the design it is a good idea to take the carving off the bench periodically and stand it upright. With some side lighting falling on the carving, you will be better able to judge how the contour effects are developing. Working with the correct cast of light can also be very useful when carving large panels in high relief, or when there are perspective elements.

Undercutting

All relief carvings rely for their effect on highlight areas, as well as shadows being cast. Highlights are the raised parts, or high spots, of the design, and are often smooth planes. The shadows are created by undercutting parts of the design. The effect is to 'lift' the design off the background, as well as removing any chunky look caused by the wood of the design being too thick. In this project undercutting was used around the leaves and flower, with just a touch added to the sides of the main stem.

Undercutting simply consists of removing part of the wood which lies behind the very edge of the design. It is achieved by making downward-slanting cuts under, for example, the edge of a leaf (Fig 8.20).

Normally the cuts are made at an angle of about 60°, inclining into the underside of the design, followed by a second cut at background level to remove the waste (Figs 8.21 and 8.22). The tools normally used are either a no. 3 gouge or a chisel, depending on the shape of the design, although from time to time the design may call for a gouge with a steeper sweep. In confined spaces a frontbent or dogleg chisel can be used to remove background waste (Fig 8.23). In low-relief work it is a mistake to attempt to undercut at too shallow an angle, as it can be difficult to remove the waste wood cleanly.

The same technique can be used to undercut the flower.

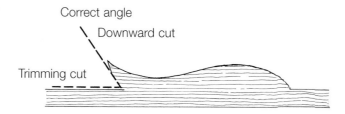

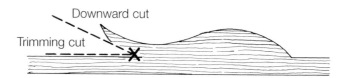

Fig 8.22 *. . . then slice off the waste wood*

Fig 8.20 *Undercut with steep downward cuts followed by trimming cuts*

Fig 8.23 *Use a dogleg chisel or a frontbent tool to undercut in confined areas*

Veining the leaves

The leaf veins can be cut with either a veiner (no. 11 gouge) or a V-tool. Usually the sub-veins on a leaf are narrower than the main vein, which means you really need at least two sizes of the no. 11 gouge. Unfortunately it is becoming increasingly difficult to buy veiners less than ¹⁄₁₆in (1.5mm) in width, and for small leaves you need to be able to cut tiny veins. For this reason many carvers opt to use the V-tool: by varying the pressure, the narrowest of veins can be achieved (Fig 8.24). Should the strokes look too harsh, they can be softened with very light sanding.

Fig 8.21 *The first stage of undercutting is to stab-cut the outline with the gouge handle held outwards at a suitable angle . . .*

Fig 8.24 *Carving leaf veins with a V-tool*

Fig 8.26 *Detail of low-relief carving used on a stool*

Fig 8.25 *The completed carving before polishing, showing the ripple-cut background*

Fig 8.27 *Low-relief carving of a leaf*

With the veining finished, and before polishing, ripple-cut the background with the ¼in (6mm) no. 3 gouge (Fig 8.25). Polishing and other finishing treatments are discussed in the next chapter. I suggest you read about them before completing this carving.

These types of floral design are very adaptable, and are particularly suitable for decorating furniture (Figs 8.26 and 8.27).

Stage-by-stage checklist for low-relief carving

1 Make certain all parts of the design can be carved with the tools you have.

2 Draw with broad lines, avoiding too much detail.

3 Match your wood to the design.

4 Mark planned carving depth on the side of the wood, and dot in your safety-net zone.

5 Cut round carbon imprint using a V-tool.

6 Remove background to the depth of the safety zone and up to the V-tool trench. Cut across grain.

7 Trim back to the design with stab-cuts, starting outside the design area to avoid stressing the wood.

8 Model the design using plenty of contours. Avoid over-use of shallow-cut gouges.

9 Undercut dominant edges of the design to increase the effect of shadows.

Project: Mirror images

The choice of subject makes this second project a natural continuation of the simple flower pattern used for the previous one. Though it takes you through more complex work, it avoids difficult situations which could easily cause you to think of giving up. This type of design is suitable as a wall plaque, or for flat panels such as a drawer front or a chair back.

Planning the design

The design shown in Fig 8.28 is based on the principle of a mirror image, with the left side being a true reflection of the right. The way to produce this type of drawing was covered briefly in Chapter 7 (pages 67–8). However, it is worth mentioning two points which always apply to mirror-image designs.

Firstly, it is vital to include locating lines in your drawing. They need to be set both horizontally and vertically, and both must pass through the centre point of the design. Similar lines need to be plotted on the carving wood. To match them up when you put the plan drawing on the wood, it is helpful to nick the paper edges (as shown by the black triangles in Fig 8.28) so you can align the two sets of lines.

Secondly, there are various ways of creating an accurate mirror image. Drawing it with a computer is a relatively simple matter if you have the appropriate software; otherwise you can do it quite easily by hand. As mentioned in Chapter 7, use either layout or tracing paper, as then you will be able to see the drawing through from the back. You only need to originate one half of the design. Then, by holding the sheet of paper up to a window with the drawing next to the glass, you can copy the design on the back. This gives you the mirror image. When you come to imprint the design onto the wood with carbon paper, use the original drawing for one half of the design and the copy on the back of the paper for the other.

Locating line

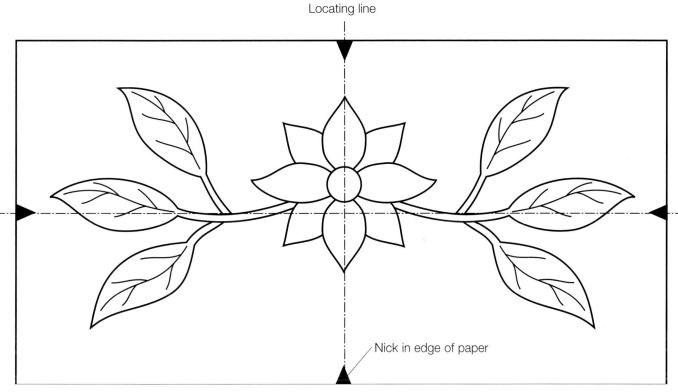

Nick in edge of paper

Fig 8.28 *This is a mirror-image drawing. When only half the design is to be drawn, use locating lines to aid in setting out the design on the wood*

Another method is to draw half the design and then use two sheets of carbon paper – one facing the wood, the other reversed to make an image on the back of the paper.

Be sure that you make the design compatible with the sizes of the tools you have, particularly in cases such as the small gaps between the leaf stems. Never draw them smaller than the smallest tool you have.

If you want your work to look really interesting, you must plan plenty of contour variation. Making a sectional drawing will help you know how the flower and its petals will have to be arranged (Fig 8.29). It will help to do the same for the leaves as well.

For ease of cutting, use lime. You will need a piece 12 x 5½ x 1in (300 x 140 x 25mm), planed flat. Hold it on a backing board, just as you did for the first project.

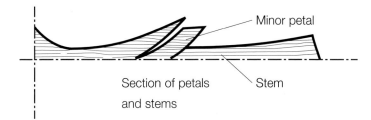

Minor petal

Section of petals
and stems

Stem

Fig 8.29 *Make sectional drawings to avoid leaving the carving flat and uninteresting*

Marking out

Fix the drawing to the wood with a strip of masking tape, making sure the locating lines are properly aligned. With carbon paper in place, overdraw the design, using a different-coloured pen to the original so as not to miss any parts of the design. Then spend a little time studying the imprint to see if changes are needed.

With every carving you do, it is essential to plot a safety net around the design to ensure you do not cut the wrong bit of wood when removing the waste. Either mark a dotted line with a felt-tip pen, or cut a trench with your V-tool (Figs 8.30 and 8.31).

Also mark the planned background depth. As in the first project, use a dotted line a little above the final depth line (Fig 8.32). Then work to the dotted line first when you take out the background.

Fig 8.32 *Marking in the background depth*

Fig 8.30 *Dot in a safety margin before starting to remove the waste*

Fig 8.33 *The waste wood can be removed with a router*

Waste removal

Start by taking out the waste with a quick-cut gouge, such as the no. 6 or no. 9 – or use a router with a flat bit (Fig 8.33). Only go down to the dotted safety line for the time being, and trim to a level background with shallow-cutting tools like the no. 4 (Fig 8.34). Check with callipers to make certain all the high spots have been removed, particularly around the design itself (Fig 8.35).

Fig 8.31 *Alternatively, cut a trench round the design with your V-tool*

Fig 8.34 *Use a shallow gouge to even the surface*

The next stage is to trim the waste back to the outline of the design. As in the first project, do this with careful stab-cuts, with the blade held perpendicularly (Fig 8.36). Use the ¼in (6mm) no. 3 and the ⅜in (9mm) no. 4 gouges, or broader versions if you have them. Avoid cutting into the background.

Cut between the leaf stems with the ¼in (6mm) no. 9, or the ¹⁄₁₆in (1.5mm) no. 11 if there is less space.

Fig 8.35 *Checking the background level with callipers*

Fig 8.36 *Stab-cutting to the outline of the design*

Plotting and shaping the contours

Even though you have planned your design with care and have a clear idea of the final look, it is still a good plan to use coloured chalks to identify the high, mid-range and low areas. Just a dab here and there is all you will need to remind you when you are carving (Fig 8.37).

Then start by setting in the lowest levels – in this case, where the main stems meet the flower – using shallow cuts with the small no. 3 gouge. By doing the low parts first you lessen the risk of running out of wood, which could easily happen if you were to carve the high areas first.

Fig 8.37 *Use coloured chalks to fix the contour levels*

Modelling

Shape the tops of the leaves to look lifelike; you do not want them to be flat. Avoid making the stems too slim at this stage, which could limit adjustment later on. You can always thin them down when the final delicacy of the work is known. Establish the shape of the flower's petals.

Use the ⅝in (15mm) no. 4, or rough-shape them with the ¼in (6mm) no. 3 and refine with the skew chisel.

Form the centre of the flower in a similar way to the previous projects, by cutting a circle with the ½in (12mm) no. 9 (Fig 8.38). (This is one of the optional tools listed in Chapter 3.) Alternatively, work the shape with the

Fig 8.38 *Starting to form the flower centre*

Fig 8.39 *Cutting the veins with the V-tool*

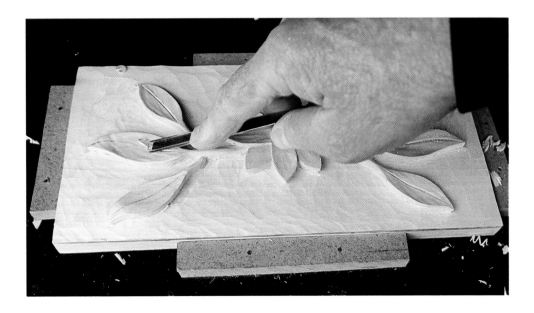

¼in (6mm) no. 3, making a series of cuts to form the circle. When you have done that, proceed to round the dome with the same no. 3 gouge, using the blade upside down. Final smoothing can be done with the no. 2 skew, or the dome can simply be sanded.

Leaf veining

Let the colour and grain you reveal dictate the final presentation of your design. This may mean deleting some aspect which seems to have become superfluous because of the way the wood now looks. In the case of the leaves, I decided to omit the minor veins as being too fussy. Only the main lateral veins were cut with the V-tool (Fig 8.39), and their edges were lightly sanded, blending them into the leaves so that they did not look contrived.

Undercutting

The flower and the leaves required undercutting to emphasize the shadow areas. The method used was the same as previously described (pages 83–4).

Sanding and finishing

There are details of how to finish and polish carvings in the next chapter. Sanding can be speeded up by the use of small pointed sticks, fashioned from bamboo garden cane (Fig 8.40), as described on page 94. Using these with small strips of sandpaper, you will be better able to access intricate parts of the design, such as in between the petals and around the leaves. The pointed part of the stick can also be used on its own to remove wisps of fibre and to burnish the wood prior to polishing.

Fig 8.41 shows the finished carving.

Summary

- **Plan out your design with regard to the size of timber available and the tools you have.**

- **Keep your tools as sharp as possible.**

- **Cut cleanly.**

- **Learn to cut sympathetically with the grain.**

- **Visualize the contours of the design.**

- **Keep the image in your mind as you carve.**

Fig 8.40 *The carving can be cleaned up with a bamboo sanding stick*

Fig 8.41 *The finished relief*

9

finishing, texturing and polishing

It is tempting to try to move quickly through the various finishing processes to achieve the end result. Unfortunately, life is just not that simple. A lot of time, effort and patience may be needed before the carving is finished. But one word of warning: when you are carrying out this work, stick to just what is required to produce a bright, clean surface. Avoid the temptation to make structural changes to the carving at this late stage.

Sanding

The aim of the carver should always be to produce a relief carving using just cutting tools. By doing so, the work will retain all the facet cuts, each of which acts as a tiny reflector to throw back light off the undulating surfaces. The resulting brightness is the hallmark of quality workmanship, and sets hand-carving apart from machine-produced work.

But in reality some sanding after cutting may be necessary. Much will depend on the carver's skill in coping with troublesome areas of grain – and, of course, on the sharpness of the gouges used. The extent of sanding usually also depends on experience: the experienced carver will only ever sand to the barest minimum, whereas the beginner is almost invariably over-zealous in the use of abrasive paper.

Sanding papers come in various grades of grit and are made from different materials (Fig 9.1). It is essential that they have flexible backings.

Aluminium oxide is often only available in the coarser grades in do-it-yourself stores. It works quickly and does not easily clog. One of the best types is coloured blue. Buy from specialist suppliers.

Silicon carbide papers (grey in colour) are ideal when the wood has been treated first with sanding sealer. They wear quickly. Foam-backed types are good for carvings. On the back of each sheet you will find a printed number, which indicates the degree of abrasiveness – the lower the number, the coarser the abrasive. For example, 40-grit sanding paper is very coarse, and 1000-grit is ultra-fine.

I usually choose medium-grade papers with a grit rating around 240 for troublesome areas, and 320-grit for rubbing down. It is always best to cut the paper into strips, rather than tearing it into pieces. Fine wire wool is frequently

Fig 9.1 *A selection of suitable abrasives*

used to smooth highlight areas, although it can cause discoloration on light woods.

Sanding should be done in the direction of the grain, and it is important to sand with single strokes as much as you can, with the lie of the grain, rather than with a back-and-forth motion which inevitably lifts the fibres on each counter-stroke. Areas which are difficult to sand, such as where the carving has been undercut, can be burnished by using a small, pointed hardwood stick (split bamboo cane is ideal) to rub the surface. This will both remove stray wisps of wood fibre and polish the surface.

If you come across patches which are difficult to cut cleanly because of their twisted grain, one solution can be to sand them down smooth and then carefully re-tool the affected surface.

Textured finishes

Textured finishes can adorn a carving and improve its general appearance, but if carried out with too much enthusiasm the effect can be both fussy and confused. If you plan to incorporate texture at any time, try out the treatment first on scrap wood.

Figs 9.2 to 9.4 illustrate how different textures can affect individual parts of a design. Note that the flower centre in Fig 9.2 has been sanded smooth, as have the petals in Fig 9.3. In both cases the effect is to deaden the

Fig 9.2 *Flower with sanded centre and original tool marks on the petals*

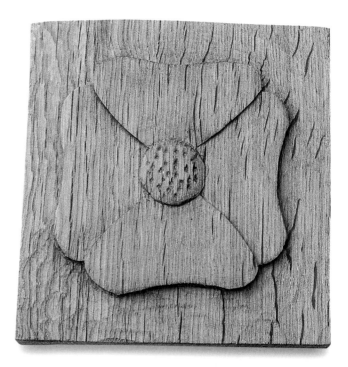

Fig 9.3 *Flower with sanded petals and nail-punch marks in the centre*

finishing, texturing and polishing

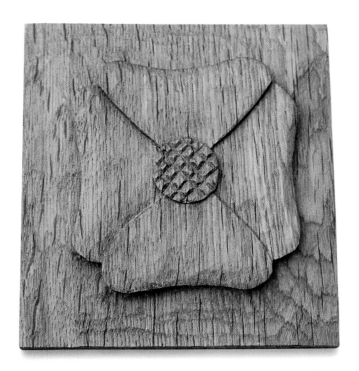

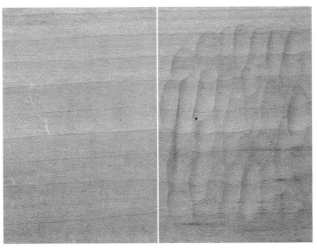

Fig 9.5 *Plain sanded background compared to a rippling background*

Fig 9.4 *Flower with lightly sanded petals and chisel cross-hatching in the centre*

look of the carving. But the petals of the flower in Fig 9.2 are shown with the original tooling cuts. These have been 'softened' by light sanding only in Fig 9.4. The chiselled cross-hatching of the central dome is very traditional.

The use of a rippling background is always preferable to a plain sanded surface (Fig 9.5), for two reasons: the

ripples act as better light reflectors when polished, and also help to disguise any flaws in the wood. The deeper the texture cuts, the greater will be their effect, because deeper shadows are produced. In Fig 9.6, for example, the veiner cuts are deeper than those made with the no. 9 gouge.

Fig 9.7 takes the example further by showing the differences between a no. 4 cut, a no. 9 cut, and that made with a no. 11 veiner. You can also see the effect of cross-hatching made with a V-tool, which is less precise than cross-hatching with a chisel.

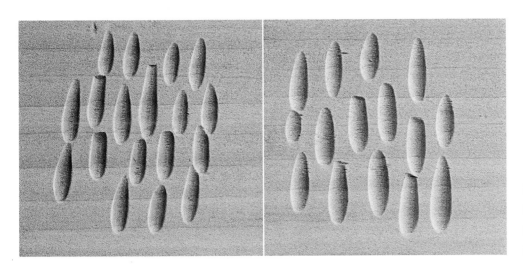

Fig 9.6 *Comparing the depth of cut obtained from a ³⁄₁₆in (5mm) veiner (left) and a no. 9 gouge*

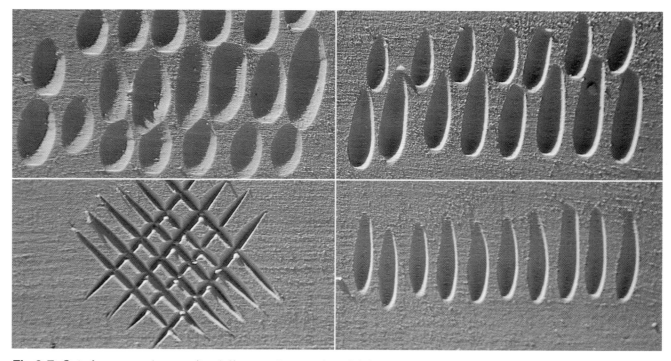

Fig 9.7 *Cuts from a no. 4 gouge* (top left)*, a no. 9 gouge* (top right) *and a no. 11 veiner* (bottom right)*, plus cross-hatching with a V-tool rather than a chisel*

Fig 9.8 shows the effects which can be created with various types of punches. Factory-made grounding punches tend to give a uniform texture and are ideal for general background work. For smaller areas quite satisfactory results can be obtained with a pozi-type cross-head screwdriver, or a nail with the point blunted.

Sealing the wood

Unless you are planning to use a stain, the next step in the finishing sequence is to seal the surface of the wood. This both hardens up the wood fibres (after sealing it is normal to sand lightly), and acts as a barrier against unwanted discoloration. The slight sheen which a sealer

Fig 9.8 *Textured finishes obtained with a factory-made punch, metal tubing, a pozi screwdriver, and a blunted nail*

gives to the surface will help you detect problem areas requiring further attention with a gouge.

Hardening the fibres may cause some to stand proud of the surface, giving a rough feel. Taking them off with light sanding is known as **de-nibbing**. Use a fine-grade abrasive paper (300 or 400 grit), and work only with the lie of the grain. Be particularly careful when sanding a ripple-cut surface: if you sand too much you may remove all the coating from the high parts and create a patchy finish.

● **Shellac sanding sealer** Shellac is easy to use, quick-drying, and soluble in methylated spirit (denatured alcohol). It is not colourless, but has a slight yellow or brown hue which imparts a pleasant, warm look to most light-coloured woods. When supplied as a sanding sealer (Fig 9.9) it also contains French chalk to act as a grain filler. Shellac is widely used for wood finishing, but it is worth remembering that it is not impervious to water and can become speckled if applied in a very damp atmosphere. Its shelf life is not particularly long, and it tends to darken with age.

● **French polish** also has a shellac base. Some carvers use it, but its brown stain can cause a patchy effect if end-grain parts of the carving are particularly absorbent.

● **Acrylic sealers** While shellac has been used for centuries, acrylic sealers are relative newcomers. They are water-soluble and extremely easy to use. An alternative to a proprietary sealer is satin-grade acrylic varnish, which is widely available in do-it-yourself stores. Dilute it with about 20% water.

Acrylic is milky-white when wet, but dries out virtually colourless, so little or no change to the hue of the wood takes place. It is thus ideal for use with very light-coloured woods such as sycamore. The only possible disadvantage is that acrylic imparts a slight plastic feel to the wood, but this is seldom noticeable when it is applied diluted. Acrylic also provides a good impervious surface.

Finishes

● **Oil finishes** Different types of oil have been used for wood finishing for centuries, but the oldest must surely be tung oil. While you can buy pure tung oil, for most needs it is far more convenient to buy a proprietary brand. In the UK, for example, Rustin's Danish Oil is widely available, and there are many others (Fig 9.10). If you follow the directions carefully it is simple to produce a satin-silk finish; but if you are too liberal with the amount of oil left on the wood to dry you will end up with a tacky coating which never hardens.

Linseed oil is another tried and tested medium. Usually the boiled type is used, diluted with a little pure turpentine. Like tung oil, linseed oil has a yellowish colour, and it also tends to darken with age.

Personally, I think oil finishes work best with brown woods, since their yellow tinge can discolour very light timbers. Their great advantage over other methods of sealing is their ability to work into all the small cut areas of a carving. Three applications are normally necessary. All oil treatments must be allowed to harden and age fully before being coated with wax polish; otherwise the surface can take on a 'bloom' rather akin to the look of oil on water.

Fig 9.9 Sanding sealer is based on shellac

Fig 9.10 One of the many proprietary brands of finishing oil

Fig 9.11 *Use a quality wax polish*

● **Wax polishing** A light coating of wax will enhance both the look and the feel of your work, as well as helping to keep it clean. Any good-quality furniture wax will be sufficient for most needs (Fig 9.11). Those containing refined beeswax cause less change to the wood colour; beeswax on its own can prove too sticky. Apply with a soft brush (a child's toothbrush will do), and work well into the cut areas. Always allow the wax to harden off before buffing with either a clean, soft brush or a lint-free natural-fibre cloth.

You can just wax bare wood, but it will take many coatings to build up a lasting surface, which is why sealers are used beforehand. The final finish of sealed wood can be improved prior to waxing if the surface is dressed with wax and rubbed down with worn fine-grade sandpaper or plastic web. For oil-treated wood, buff with plastic web lubricated with a few drops of finishing oil.

But no matter which treatment you decide to use, do remember two vital points. Firstly, no amount of waxing will miraculously turn a badly produced carving into a masterpiece. The reverse is true: poorly cut work will stand out even more. So do keep in mind that the quality of the final finish depends completely on the skill used to cut the wood in the first place, plus the time and patience employed in preparing the work for waxing.

Secondly, aim at all times for a *sheen* and not a shine. The patina acquired by old furniture is the product of years of caring, and doesn't happen overnight. It takes time for oils and waxes to mature and interact with the wood resins, and naturally, if the wood has been sealed with an impervious barrier, such as acrylic, this will not happen. Science has yet to come up with a 'quick-fix' treatment. A coating of wax applied sparingly at maybe three- or six-month intervals will be far more effective in the long term than too much too soon. Excessive waxing or oiling just creates an anaerobic layer which prevents most of the coating ever drying out fully.

Summary

● Spend plenty of time preparing the surface before finishing. Try to eradicate any poorly cut parts, but avoid structural changes at this stage.

● Choose the type of sealer with regard to the colour of the wood. Light woods respond well to either shellac or acrylic. Brown woods work well with an oil finish.

● Sand with care, using worn fine-grade paper, after the first sealing coat is fully dry.

● Burnish with a hardwood stick to remove traces of fibres, especially in undercut areas.

● Wax is used for the final finish after sealing with shellac or acrylic, or after using oil. It is best to let an oil finish mature for a week or more before using any wax.

10 carving in high relief

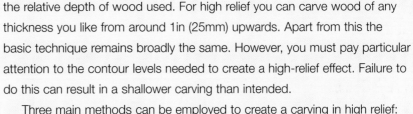

The main difference between a low-relief carving and one in high relief is the relative depth of wood used. For high relief you can carve wood of any thickness you like from around 1in (25mm) upwards. Apart from this the basic technique remains broadly the same. However, you must pay particular attention to the contour levels needed to create a high-relief effect. Failure to do this can result in a shallower carving than intended.

Three main methods can be employed to create a carving in high relief: working in thick timber, the applied technique, or the appliqué method.

● **Thick timber** For your first attempts at high-relief carving you may wish to use quite thick timber. Dramatic high-relief carvings can be produced from 4in (100mm) timber, which gives a good grain 'flow' to the design. You could use even larger pieces, with a back-to-front depth of up to 12in (300mm), provided they are hollowed out at the back to prevent splitting. The timber at the centre of a really thick piece will have a higher moisture content than the edges, so hollowing out the back helps to balance out the thickness of the wood and reduce the effects of any subsequent expansion or contraction.

● **Applied technique** At one time this method was widely used for all forms of decorative carving. It works on the principle of building up the levels needed using blocks of wood, which can be pre-cut or even partially carved. When the blocks are glued together it is usual to reverse and stagger the annual ring configuration to balance out any inherent stress (Fig. 10.1). The applied technique was extensively used for heavy and ornate work, most of which was then gilded.

But problems can occur when various segments of wood expand or contract at different rates, meaning that eventually the joints will show. The visual effect can also be marred by breaks in the flow of the grain, which is bound to happen when pieces of timber are glued together. For these reasons you may find it more satisfactory to work in a single piece of thick timber rather than using the applied technique, unless your design is particularly large and ornate.

Fig 10.1 *Annual rings are*
reversed and staggered
when building up a high-
relief carving, to balance
the inherent stresses in
the wood

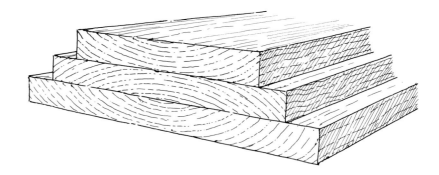

● **Appliqué furniture decoration** While the building-block method of the applied technique is fine for architectural work, it is less suitable for decorating furniture, especially as heavy and ornate carving is seldom required nowadays. A simplified version of the technique has evolved for use when a deep carving is needed to decorate a piece of furniture – a decorative shell, perhaps, or a heraldic shield. The embellishment is carved first as a separate entity, and then simply glued on (Fig 10.2).

This avoids the problem of having to remove considerable quantities of valuable wood when the furniture is made – as you would using the normal relief-carving method – which could either weaken the furniture or mean using far thicker wood than otherwise required. It also has the advantage that the decorative carving need not necessarily be of the same wood as the furniture, but can be stained to match. You can thus select suitable timber for both your furniture and your carving, thereby avoiding the problem of carving an intricate pattern in wood which is not capable of accepting fine detail. Mouldings are often applied in the same way, just as a do-it-yourself enthusiast might use pre-formed mouldings to enhance a plain door.

The basic outline shape is usually pre-formed. The carving wood can be secured to a backing board, or to the bench, by screwing from behind – you need to make sure that the screws are in the thick part of the carving. Alternatively, you can glue the carving wood to the backing board with water-soluble glue. Sandwich a sheet of paper between the block and the backing board, or bench, to aid removal (Fig 10.3). You can carve the entire piece on the backing board, or simply form the basic outline and then do the final modelling when you have glued the decoration to the furniture.

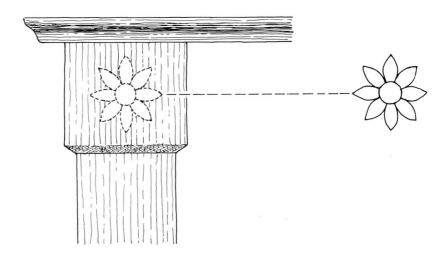

Fig 10.2 *Carved design*
applied to furniture using
the appliqué technique

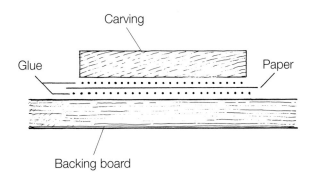

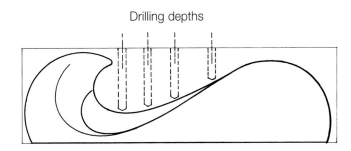

Fig 10.3 Sandwich paper between the carving and the
backing board to aid removal

Background removal

Working in high relief does, of course, necessitate the
removal of considerable quantities of waste material, and
there are several different methods of doing this.

In the case of a simple design it is best to use the
process described in the low-relief project. The design
is put onto the wood with carbon paper, outlined with a
V-tool, and then the surrounding wood removed by
sawing, routing, or just gouge cutting. Although this can
be a little tedious, especially if the wood is very thick,
it does ensure that the design area is left untouched until
modelling starts, and is thus the recommended method
for your initial attempts at high relief.

But as your skill increases it may help to know about
alternative methods of background removal. If you are
planning a more complex pattern incorporating small and
delicate areas – a shield, for example, or a deeply carved
flower with a number of different levels – the problem is
how to dig deeply in a confined space.

In this case it is better to create the main contours
first, and then re-apply the design. This usually means
having to draw freehand, since invariably a paper pattern
will distort when curved. But by sketching a grid of lines
onto the wood after the initial shaping, you can help to
locate your freehand drawing.

Another method is to fix the approximate location of
the intricate parts by drilling out some of the surrounding

Fig 10.4 Removing waste wood with a drill, using a
depth gauge to ensure the drilling ends just above the final
carving level

waste wood. Use a drill with a depth gauge to ensure the
holes are kept shallower than the final background level
(Fig 10.4).

A flexible approach

Pictorial scenes may be carved better if you do not
remove all the background at the outset, but leave some
latitude for gauging perspective and adding to the design
if required. As long as you leave enough spare wood
during the roughing-out process, you will have flexibility.

For example, imagine carving a wall plaque depicting a
school of dolphins leaping through the waves. Initially, you
might be satisfied with drawing all or part of their bodies
as seen at surface level. Later, though, as you develop the
carving, it may seem a good idea to include some detail
below the waterline, to expand the interest of the work
and allow you to use different techniques to create the
effect. You might even decide to include a sunset at wave
level, or some marine creatures on the sea bed.

If all or most of the background wood is removed too rapidly, as it might be if a router is used, you could find you just have not the wood left to indulge these artistic fancies. But if you only remove the waste wood immediately surrounding the dominant parts of the design – in this example, the main dolphins – you would have plenty of material available to add the extra detail.

It is thus essential to keep the design fluid when carrying out this type of work, and only remove sufficient wood as and when required. Let the design evolve as you go along. Probably much of the very ornate and complex carving of yesteryear was carried out like this.

Project: Carving a boss

The wood used for this carving was 2in (50mm) thick oak. Normally the whole carving would be worked stage by stage, but in this example each leaf has received varying amounts of development to illustrate the progression of the work (Fig 10.5).

Fig 10.5 *The four leaves show the four stages of development in carving this high-relief boss*

Reading from the leaf at top left, the carving sequence can be followed easily. At the top left (1) the leaf areas have been marked out using a V-tool. In the top right leaf (2) the contour levels have been set in. The bottom right leaf (3) shows a later stage in establishing the contour levels; note the veiner cuts on the main part of the leaf for the ridge. The bottom left segment (4) shows the completed leaf.

Due to the narrow gaps between the four leaves, the best way to remove waste wood is to use a router. Care is needed to avoid burning the wood or overheating the cutter, which means taking a succession of shallow cuts down to the final depth of 1in (25mm). Note that if you stop the depth of cut fractionally above the required measurement, you can finish off with gouge ripple-cuts.

Two other methods could be used to remove the waste wood. It can be taken out with gouges, but in that case wider divisions might be needed between the leaves to facilitate cutting. Alternatively, using the appliqué technique, the design could be pre-cut from 1in (25mm) timber and then glued in place.

Project: Floral plaque

The wood used in this project was 2in (50mm) thick sweet chestnut, and the elliptical shape of the plaque measured 11¾ by 7⅝in (295 x 195mm). (Guidance on drawing an ellipse can be found in the Appendix, page 142.)

Modelling in clay

After the drawing had been completed, including sectional shapes (Fig 10.6), the design was modelled in clay (Fig 10.7). You can make alterations easily, and the model will help considerably in determining the number and depth of levels needed to create the design effectively.

Tracing the design

The design is then drawn on the wood using carbon paper, after which you should check to see if any

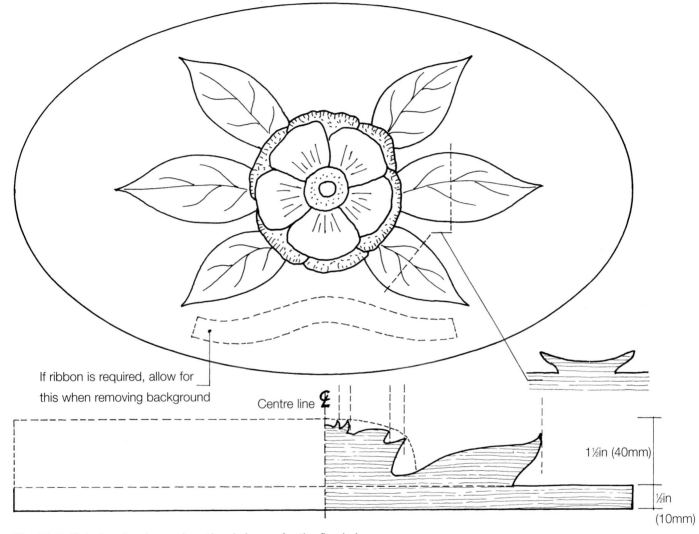

If ribbon is required, allow for
this when removing background

Centre line

1½in (40mm)

½in

(10mm)

Fig 10.6 *Flat plan drawing and sectional shapes for the floral plaque*

Fig 10.7 *Clay model of high-relief floral plaque*

alterations are needed. These are often only apparent
when you see the design on the wood. For example, note
the difference in the width of the leaves between my
original drawing and Fig 10.8.

The depth of the background was set at about ⅛in
(10mm) and marked on the edge of the panel, along with
the usual dotted safety net to prevent too much wood
being removed. Because of its elliptical shape, the carving
was screwed to the backing board with three no. 8
screws, making sure the screws did not penetrate the
wood as far as the thickness of the background (Fig 10.9).

Fig 10.8 *The design drawn on the wood; the leaves are now wider and closer together than in the drawing*

Fig 10.10 *Large areas of waste wood can be cut away with a saw*

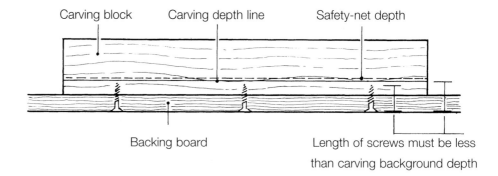

Fig 10.9 *Screwing the carving to the backing board without penetrating the background*

Carving block   Carving depth line   Safety-net depth

Backing board   Length of screws must be less than carving background depth

Outlining and wasting away

Next the design outline was cut with a no. 39 V-tool, working in the waste on the outside of the drawn line as described in Chapter 8. The waste background wood can be removed simply with gouge cuts, in the same way as for a low-relief carving. Do not be daunted by the amount of wood which needs to be removed, but be careful not to overstress the wood by using excessive force. Stressing the wood causes internal fractures,

which may not become apparent until the modelling is started, so just make moderately light cuts.

Larger waste areas can be removed with a saw (Fig 10.10), but saw cuts must go no deeper than just above the dotted safety-depth line (Fig 10.11). Go any deeper than this, and you may have score marks in the final background. Waste can also be removed with a router (Fig 10.12), again working to just above the dotted safety-net line.

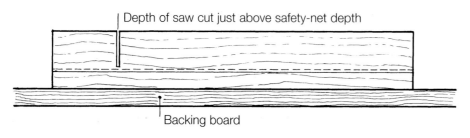

Depth of saw cut just above safety-net depth

Backing board

Fig 10.11 *Take care to stop saw cuts just above the dotted safety line, to avoid scoring the background*

Fig 10.12 *Using a router to remove waste wood*

Setting in

Setting in the design is done in the same way as for low-relief work, by reducing the wood back to the design lines. The height of the leaves must be established, below the level of the flower. At this stage the leaves can be kept reasonably flat, so their surfaces can be cut with a no. 3 gouge; but later they will need to be modelled realistically using no. 6 and no. 9 gouges. The division of the leaves at the point where they join the flower can be cut with a no. 2 skew chisel. Set in the ribbon, making the wood slightly thicker than will be finally required. Fig 10.13 shows the leaves and ribbon roughly set in and ready for detailed modelling.

The initial cutting of the flower petals is, again, similar to the method used in low-relief carving: the petals are defined with V-tool cuts on their low-level sides. But the essential difference in this project is that they are arranged in two definite groups, with five upper petals lying on top of the other, lower petals. Though the clay model shows their arrangement, a sectional sketch may provide greater clarification (Fig 10.14).

Fig 10.13 *The design is now set in the wood, ready for modelling to begin*

The top petals

After V-cutting the outline of all the petals, fix them by shaping the bottom ones with no. 3 and no. 6 gouges before working on the top five. Fig 10.15 shows the initial carving on the lower petals and leaves, while the top petals have been marked with a letter H to show their high spots. You can see how the flower centre is being lowered

105

Upper petals
Lower petals
Leaves
Background
Backing board

*Fig 10.14 Schematic
cross section showing the
various levels of petals,
leaves and background.
The carving is made in one
piece, not laminated*

*Fig 10.15 Forming the
flower centre, having
already worked the leaves
and lower petals*

with a no. 5 gouge to expose the highest point of the
central detail. The method is similar to that used in the
low-relief project: vertical stab-cuts form the central ring.

The small dome in the centre is marked in with a ¼in
(6mm) no. 9 gouge and rounded over using an inverted
¼in (6mm) no. 3. The ring depicting the flower's stamens
is then cut and shaped with the ½in (12mm) no. 6 gouge
(Fig 10.16). The definition of the upper petals will gradually
be lost as this work progresses, so set them in repeatedly
with further stab cuts.

When carrying out all this central work it is essential to
remove sufficient wood to ensure that the upper petals will
dip in realistically towards the middle. This will also ensure

sufficient access space to allow you to shape and
undercut the stamen ring.

Take care, though, not to cut so deep that straight-
bladed tools become inoperative because of their angle
of entry. A depth of ⅜in (10mm) from the high points
of the petals to the base of the central dome should
be sufficient.

Modelling the petals

The shaping of the petal contours is done using both
the no. 6 and the ¼in (6mm) no. 9 gouges. Cut with care,
as the total effect of the carving can easily be marred by
mistakes at this stage. Try to visualize the liveliness of the

Fig 10.16 *Shaping and setting down the ring of stamens with a no. 6 gouge*

natural flower, and exercise the maximum amount of undulation, combined with downward-rolling edges in places where the tips fall on cross grain. Moderately undercut the petals.

By this stage in the carving you should have become aware not only of the general character of the wood, such as the lie of the grain and whether or not it is capable of accepting delicate detail, but also of any problem areas. The most common troublesome features are patches of twisted or interlocked grain, which limit your choice of cutting direction. You may well need to make modifications to the design, since these areas will certainly require a stronger and more robust style of work.

In my carving, for example, one area of the wood was wild and twisted. Not only did this mean that virtually all the cutting had to be at right angles to the length of the carving and the 'flow' of the design, but also that leaf shaping had to be done with extreme care to prevent bits of wood breaking off. I had to adjust the direction of cut frequently to compensate for the twist in the grain.

Fig 10.17 shows the start of one such cut, and Fig 10.18 shows the gouge position at the end of the stroke, by which time the cutting direction has changed. At the start of the cut the blade edge is square on to the wood; by the end of the stroke it is tilted.

Fig 10.17 *Starting a cut in an area of twisted grain, with the gouge blade square to the wood*

Fig 10.18 *Finishing the same cut, with the blade tilted as the direction of cut has been altered to run with the lie of the grain*

Modelling the leaves

Once contour modelling is under way, it is vital to stand the carving on its lower edge at frequent intervals and check the visual effect. The thickness of the wood left after the initial setting-in gives scope for producing leaves with plenty of twist and curl. Avoid any temptation to retain their flat image by carving them with a gouge shallower than a no. 6, and work with this tool throughout the leaf modelling to create lots of 'movement'. You will need to view the carving from the sides as much as from above to make full use of the depth of timber.

Undercutting

The leaves are undercut to increase the shadow effect, but make sure you do not cut downwards at too shallow an angle. Fig 10.19 shows the angle to use. There is no need to try to create a three-dimensional form, as this would only weaken the carving unnecessarily. With more close-grained wood (lime, for example, rather than the chestnut I used here), more undercutting can be used.

Fig 10.19 *Undercutting the leaves; be sure to cut at a reasonably steep angle*

Interpretation of details

Interpretation of any leaf veining is a personal matter, and you will find it helpful at this stage to examine a real leaf carefully. Note that the veins usually lie in a shallow trench on the top side of the leaf, but on the underside they stand out. Unlike low-relief work, where scope of expression may be limited by the amount of wood available, in high relief the carver should have plenty of opportunity for personal interpretation and expression.

But it is worth noting that visual impact can be lost if some parts of the work contain too much intricate detail, especially if the grain and figuring of the wood are very evident. Chestnut can best be described as a 'bold' wood, with visually strong grain lines; and this grain will certainly reduce, or even negate, the effect of much minor detail. In this instance, I therefore chose to use only one central vein on each leaf.

The trough is created first, using the ¼in (6mm) no. 9 gouge. The outer edges of the trough are then blended into the leaf surface with a no. 3 gouge. Then the line of the vein is set in with the ⅟₁₆in (1.5mm) no. 11 veiner (Fig 10.20), and the edges again blended into the trough. To do this last blending you can use either the no. 3 gouge (Fig 10.21) or abrasive paper. Fig 10.22 summarizes the whole sequence of veining the leaves.

Fig 10.20 *Forming the leaf veins with a no. 11 veiner*

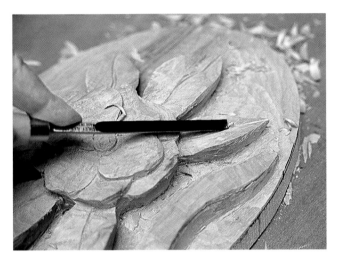

Fig 10.21 *Blending the edges of the vein into the trough with a no. 3 gouge*

Form trough with no. 9 gouge and blend outer edges to leaf surface using no. 3 gouge

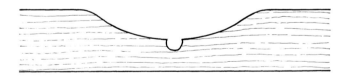

Cut vein with no. 11 gouge

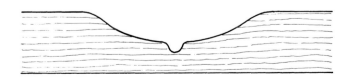

Blend edges of vein to trough surface using no. 3 gouge, or use abrasive paper

Fig 10.22 *Step-by-step sequence of creating a leaf vein*

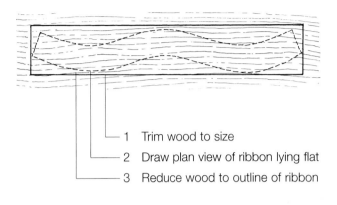

1 Trim wood to size

2 Draw plan view of ribbon lying flat

3 Reduce wood to outline of ribbon

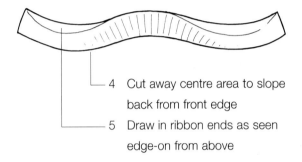

4 Cut away centre area to slope back from front edge

5 Draw in ribbon ends as seen edge-on from above

Undercut these areas

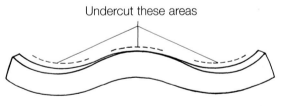

6 Trim and cut ends to blend in with central curve; undercut as shown

Fig 10.23 *Step-by-step guide to carving the ribbon detail*

The ribbon

After completing the flower and leaves, work the small ribbon. Trim the wood to size and shape in block form, ignoring the twists in the ribbon at this stage. Then tilt the central portion back from the front edge using angled cuts. Finally, undercut the ends of the ribbon steeply from behind and blend them into the central portion (Fig 10.23).

Fuming the wood

As chestnut is a wood containing tannic acid, I decided to fume the carving to darken its colour. But since no cutting work is ever possible after fuming, for fear of revealing the natural colour again, it is essential first to ensure that no parts need tidying up. Similarly, any sanding must be done before fuming – although only minimal sanding should be necessary if the wood has been cut correctly with sharp tools. I used crumpled 500-grit paper rubbed gently to remove any rough areas and blend in sharp edges (Fig 10.24), and a pointed stick to burnish undercut areas and remove stray fibres (Fig 10.25).

To fume the carving, I used two small pieces of wood to raise the carving and allow the vapour to come into contact with the back surface; a shallow container for the ammonia solution; and an old garden cloche to provide a reasonably air-tight cover (Fig 10.26). Using a cloche, or similar clear plastic cover, enables you to check the colour change without lifting up the cover and losing the ammonia vapour. It is best to stand everything on a plastic surface while fuming actually takes place. I wanted the carving to darken to a shade similar to that of dark walnut, which took about two hours. After fuming, the grain

Fig 10.25 *Burnishing undercut areas with a pointed stick*

Fig 10.26 *The equipment required for fuming, with a piece of natural wood placed beside the fumed carving to show the colour change achieved*

may have been raised in some areas, so sand it back very gently with fine-grade paper. (For more on fuming, see pages 134–5.)

Applying the finish

The final treatments involved applying three coats of Danish oil, gently burnishing the wood with plastic web between coats. After the last coat had dried and matured for a few days, I applied wax polish with a soft toothbrush and buffed it with a soft, dry brush. You can see the end result in Fig 10.27.

Fig 10.24 *Gently removing rough areas with crumpled sandpaper*

Fig 10.27

*The completed carving
after finishing and treating*

Summary

- Use good-quality timber which is capable of taking detail.

- Use wood 3–4in (75–100mm) thick for your first carving.

- Plan out the design carefully to avoid mistakes. Correcting errors can reduce the relief effect.

- Make a preliminary model in clay or other modelling material.

- When using a saw to remove waste, end the cut well above the final background depth to avoid score marks.

- Do not cut with a router to the final background depth, but leave enough wood to allow ripple-cutting with a gouge.

- Avoid using shallow-cut gouges too extensively.

- Think of the contours continually as you are carving, and visualize the subject in all its three dimensions.

- Set in the lowest design elements as early on as you can, to avoid the carving becoming deeper than planned – unless you are doing a pictorial scene requiring a more flexible approach.

Project: Beads and berries

There is often a need to carve detail which is both round in outline and convex in sectional shape. Berries are a typical example, and others include the centre of a flower, or a link of decorative beads. As the cutting sequence is the same in all cases, the method described here for berries can be taken to apply to virtually any other rounded (convex) form (Fig 10.28).

Marking out

First you need to mark out the circles needed for the outline shape. There are different ways this can be done. You could start by drawing circles with a compass, or even just sketch their position in with a pencil. But I prefer to mark their size and position more permanently.

I use a hollow punch (Fig 10.29) to set in the outline circles I need. You can make a suitable marker from copper tube. This will ensure all your berries are the same size.

However, with a little practice you will find a half-round no. 9 gouge will scribe circles perfectly well (Fig 10.30). A ½in (12mm) no. 9 is ideal. Remember, though, that the cuts of all gouges up to no. 8 are based on arcs of circles, so in effect they will all cut rings of one size or another.

Start by setting in the rings you will need. Do this by making light stab-cuts, holding the gouge upright and tapping gently with a mallet, twisting the tool round in a circle as you go. Then deepen the cuts with more force, taking care not to split the grain at all.

When you have stab-cut the rings as deeply as you reasonably can, start rounding the tops to shape the domes. Note that this must be done with the blade inverted (Fig 10.31). Whilst at first you may still be able to use the no. 9, as the modelling progresses you will have to change to a shallow-cutting gouge like the small no. 3, or the no. 5. The reason is that the corners of a standard no. 9 will soon start to dig into the sides of the domes.

As you continue the modelling stage you will need to make further downward stab cuts with the no. 9, or with

Fig 10.28 *A cluster of carved berries*

Fig 10.29 *A selection of hollow punches*

Fig 10.31 *Shaping the domes; note that the inside edge of the gouge is facing the wood surface*

Fig 10.30 *Using a half-round gouge to mark out the position of a group of berries*

the hollow punch first used, until you reach the required depth for the detail to be completed.

Whilst it is possible to complete carving the berries with the no. 3 or no. 5 gouges, you will get a better finish if the final rounding is done with a skew chisel. This tool is also ideal to clear away surplus wood between the berries (Fig 10.32).

Fig 10.32 *Using a skew chisel to round the domes and clean between them*

11 carving flat surfaces

We turn now to the techniques which can be employed to decorate a surface which of necessity must remain flat. You may want to carve a chair seat or backrest, or perhaps the corners of a table top. Normal relief treatment is clearly unsuitable: sitting on a chair embellished with a bumpy carving would be worse than sitting on a pebbly beach! In these situations you can use other methods to produce a pattern which is cut, or **incised**, into the surface of the wood.

Incised carving

You will find examples of basic incised carving on old furniture – especially chair seats and backs, and edges of table tops – for it was a popular and inexpensive way of decoration. These days at craft fairs you may well come across country-style coffee tables with rustic scenes carved in the incised method. It can be a most attractive technique, and is equally suited to producing pictorial wall plaques.

   In its simplest form, incised carving consists of cutting only with a V-tool. Just think of producing a line drawing, but using the V-tool instead of a pencil. It is as simple as that – or nearly so, since obviously you won't be able to erase any mistakes. All you need to carry out this work is a sharp V-tool and good-quality timber; and working with just a V-tool will teach you a lot about good tool control.

● **Design considerations** It is better to use flowing lines rather than an angular pattern incorporating straight lines, since great care is needed to cut a truly straight line through grain of varying density. The carving shown in Fig 11.1 was worked mainly with a V-tool, and then a slight amount of low-relief modelling was applied. If you want to carve a pictorial wall plaque like this, pick a subject which is not over-complicated, and use the no. 39 V-tool.

● **Technique basics** Incised carvings are normally cut using a regular V-trench along the design line. For greater accuracy it is best to work with a mallet, using light taps and taking short strokes. This helps you to cut to an even depth – seldom more than ⅛in (3mm) – and reduces the chance of the tool skating off the design and spoiling the surrounding wood. But if you wish to add emphasis to any part of the design, angle the tool to one side or the other to increase the amount of reflected light. This technique was used to carve some parts of Fig 11.1. Try as far as possible to cut on a shallow angle to the run of the grain, which will give a cleaner cut.

At the intersection of two lines, stop one just short of the other on either side of the crossing point. The effect will be better than if you plough through the first cut line. Your drawing will guide you as to which should be the dominant line, and the decision is normally quite simple.

Before commencing carving, make sure the surface is well prepared. If the incised lines are to be coloured, seal the wood before carving. (For further information on colouring wood see Chapter 13.)

Modified incised carving

You can take the incised method further by using what I call the 'modified' technique. This involves cutting the outline with a V-tool, then modelling the design slightly to create shallow contours. However, it is essential not to confuse this technique with low-relief carving. The crucial difference is that the background is not removed at any time, and the depth of cut is seldom greater than ⅛–³⁄₁₆in (3–4.5mm). Restraint must always be used when cutting the contours, or you will be back to sitting on that pebble beach!

Modified incised carving has much to commend it as a means of creating simple yet effective decoration. It is an ideal treatment for timber which, because of its hardness or poor inter-cell bonding, may be difficult to carve in normal relief.

Fig 11.1 *Incised carving by the late W. J. C. Quennell*

Fig 11.2 *Typical design using the modified incised carving technique*

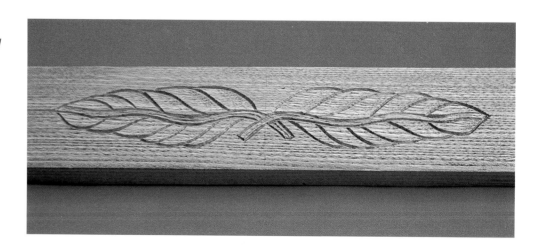

Figs 11.2 and 11.3 show a typical example of the technique, suitable for a chair back, drawer front or table rail. One half of the design could be used to decorate a cabriole leg. A floral pattern carved in this manner would be perfect for a stool top. Note that the design is a mirror image: the left portion is a reverse of the right-hand side. Only one half needed to be drawn; the paper was reversed to make the second image (see pages 67–8).

● **Incising the outline** The carving was carried out with a ¼in (6mm) V-tool, a ½in (12mm) no. 6 gouge, a ¼in (6mm) no. 9 gouge, and a ¹⁄₁₆in (1.5mm) no. 11 veiner (all tools included in the recommended first

purchase list on page 33). The V-tool was used first, to incise all the design lines by cutting a shallow trench (Fig 11.4). Note that this tool is used for incising the basic outline shape as well as each leaf segment.

In this style of carving the centre vein of the leaf is not usually shown as just an incised line, as it is for normal relief work. A better effect is achieved by cutting the outline with two parallel grooves, using a V-tool (Fig 11.5), allowing sufficient width to cut a small depression along the middle of the vein with a no. 11 gouge. This technique improves light reflection from the surface of the design, and is also used for stems. The effect, in cross section, is shown in Fig 11.6.

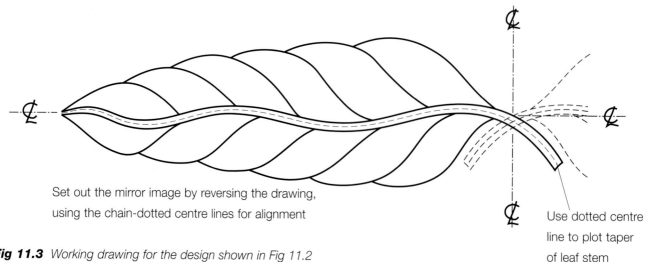

Set out the mirror image by reversing the drawing, using the chain-dotted centre lines for alignment

Use dotted centre line to plot taper of leaf stem

Fig 11.3 *Working drawing for the design shown in Fig 11.2*

Fig 11.4 *Cutting the outline with a V-tool*

Fig 11.5 *The centre vein is delineated by V-grooves on either side*

Groove along centre line of stem

Fig 11.6 *Cross section along the centre of an incised stem, showing the groove used to improve light reflection*

● **Adding the contour modelling** Each segment of the leaves is hollowed out slightly; provided the cutting is not too deep, you can produce pleasing contours while still retaining a reasonably flat surface. These contours add considerably to the overall appearance of the work. A no. 6 gouge is suitable for shallow contours, but when using a shallow gouge there is always a risk of the side walls coming into contact with the wood and causing splits. To prevent this happening, it is best to make the first cuts with a deep gouge, such as the no. 9, to ensure the sides are well above the level of the wood (Fig 11.7). These cuts can then be blended out to the edges of the leaf segment using the no. 6 gouge.

Care is needed to ensure each cut is made in sympathy with the lie of the grain, which may mean making a short test cut in one direction (Fig 11.8), then reversing the cut the other way if the grain shows any

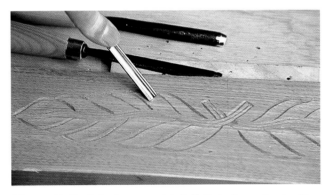

Fig 11.7 *Each leaf segment is initially hollowed out with a no. 9 gouge*

sign of tearing (Fig 11.9). Cutting sympathetically with the grain flow is, of course, fundamental to all forms of carving. But whereas with normal relief work you often have the chance to rectify a mistake by lowering the wood a touch, the shallow depth of the modified incised

Fig 11.8 *Make a test cut to check the lie of the grain . . .*

Fig 11.9 *. . . then reverse the cut if the grain starts to tear*

method means you seldom find any wood to spare (Fig 11.10). Each cut has to be just right first time – but don't be put off by this, as it is good practice.

Fig 11.11 shows the minor stem lowered to give the impression of passing under the major stem. This necessitates only a slight change of level, made by dipping the minor stem on either side of the intersection point.

● **Finishing the surfaces** Sanding should always be kept to a minimum in this kind of work; otherwise the sharpness of the cut lines may be lost. You should never need to use paper coarser than 500 grit, and worn abrasive paper is best, as its cutting action is reduced. Worn paper is also easy to scrunch into a ball for working into depressions.

Fig 11.10 *A straightedge reveals the shallowness of the contour cutting*

Intaglio carving

Intaglio work simply means creating reversed images. You will find it whenever a hollowed-out design is needed: making a mould, for example, or printing white on black. The intaglio method can be extremely useful in decorative carving, not least because it is relatively quick and easy. Fig 11.12 shows a flower cut with just a few strokes of a no. 9 gouge. In this instance the wood has first been stained to provide a clearer illustration, but in practice the petals would probably be darkened.

Fig 11.11 *One stem appears to pass under the other. Note how the centre of the stem has been grooved with a veiner for added light reflection*

Fig 11.12 *A simple intaglio flower design*

Intaglio carving is also a good technique to use if you are faced with carving delicate detail in wood which is either very coarse or has lots of interlocked grain. You can only ever carve to the capability of the timber, and in these circumstances the chances are that sooner or later parts of the design will split and break off if you use the normal relief technique. But if you use the intaglio method the design is switched to a negative image, so the high parts of the design become low parts, and there are no delicate high-level details to snap off.

● **Tools and technique** Just as with the modified incised technique, careful and precise cutting is vital in intaglio carving. Fig 11.13 shows the flat plan of a leaf to be carved, and Figs 11.14 and 11.15 show the initial cutting sequence. Note that the no. 11 veiner is used for the outlining stage: the round-bottomed cut of the veiner is easier to blend into the leaf shape than the sharp cut of a V-tool. Remember to cut *inside* the design lines.

Intaglio carving is ideal when the wood will not take raised detail. Use it also for outdoor signs, as it is less vulnerable to weather damage.

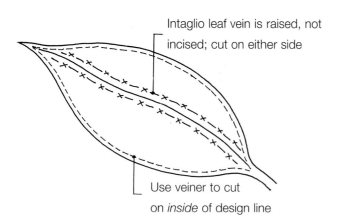

Intaglio leaf vein is raised, not incised; cut on either side

Use veiner to cut on *inside* of design line

Fig 11.13 *Flat plan of leaf to be carved in the intaglio method*

The main depressions are formed with a deep gouge, such as a no. 9, so the blade edges do not tear out any wood (Fig 11.16). If you carve carefully you can achieve quite an even surface; any remaining marks will provide useful texture, so little or no sanding should be needed (Fig 11.17). Only straight-bladed tools are normally required for intaglio cutting on flat surfaces. Try to avoid a design involving really deep impressions unless you have spoon-shaped gouges.

Fig 11.14 *Use a veiner to outline the intaglio design . . .*

Fig 11.15 *. . . and to form the central vein*

Fig 11.16 *Forming the main depressions in the leaf with a no. 9 gouge*

Fig 11.18 shows the final leaf carved as a reverse image in the wood, and can also illustrate a curious aspect of intaglio work. Depending on how the light falls on its surface, the carving may have a *trompe-l'œil* effect of appearing to protrude from the surface of the wood rather than being recessed into it. You may even have difficulty in 'reading' the photographs of intaglio work in this book as being recessed rather than raised carvings. It is simply a trick of the light, and turning the book upside down may help you to see the reversed image.

Fig 11.17 *Shallow gouge marks are left to give texture to the carving*

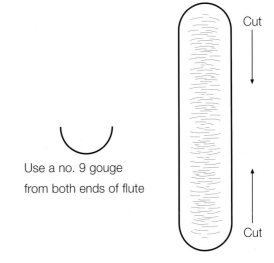

Use a no. 9 gouge
from both ends of flute

Avoid cutting to full gouge depth

Fig 11.19 *A simple flute*

Fig 11.18 *The finished intaglio-carved leaf*

Flutes

Flutes are a popular method of decorating a flat surface such as the rails found below a table top. This type of decoration was also popular for the fronts of chests. There are basically two ways they can be carved:

Fig 11.19 shows the simplest form of flute. It can be cut with a quick-cut gouge, such as the no. 9, worked from both directions. In appearance it is not dissimilar to flutes cut with a router, which is a drawback.

A better method is shown in Fig 11.20. This has a no. 5 stab-cut at the lower end of the flute. This immediately shows it has been hand-carved, not machine-cut.

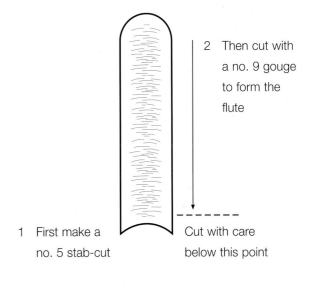

2 Then cut with a no. 9 gouge to form the flute

1 First make a no. 5 stab-cut

Cut with care below this point

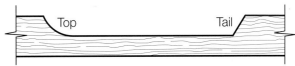

Fig 11.20 *A more sophisticated flute*

Fig 11.21 *Alternating flutes with other decorative cuts*

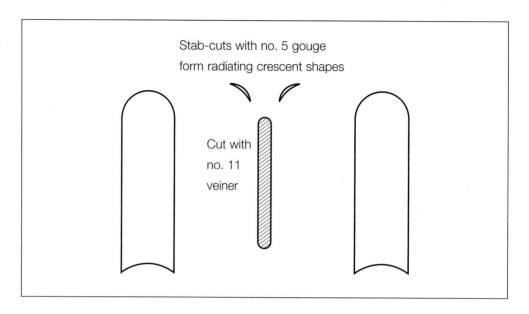

Stab-cuts with no. 5 gouge form radiating crescent shapes

Cut with no. 11 veiner

A further variation is shown in Fig 11.21. Here the flutes are interspersed with smaller troughs cut with a no. 11 veiner. Further embellishment can then be added above the tops of these troughs by way of crescent-shaped stab-cuts made with a no. 5 gouge.

Fig 11.22 *Sequence of cuts used in chip carving*

Fig 11.23 *A typical traditional chip-carved design*

A Draw three concentric circles

B Decide number of segments, then divide this number into 360° to calculate angle of each segment

C Mark in tips of segments

D Stab-cut outline of tips, and short segment lines

E Using no. 3 gouge, remove waste to outer circle

F Stab-cut the troughs deeper at front; cut the facets at an angle; inner circle can be rounded over

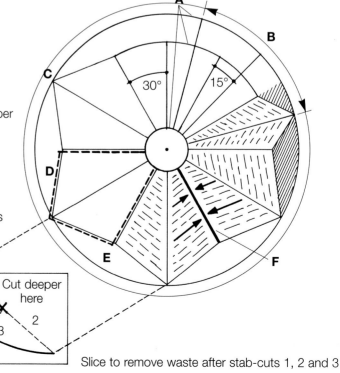

Cut deeper here

Slice to remove waste after stab-cuts 1, 2 and 3

Chip carving

This technique of cutting designs with defined angles has been widely used for centuries. Historians attribute its origin in the western world to parts of Scandinavia, although similar methods were clearly used by primitive man in many other areas. During the latter part of the nineteenth century chip carving became very popular. It was a favourite hobby for Victorian ladies to decorate box lids in this way, or in fact any small wooden article capable of being carved by hand with geometric designs.

● **Tools and technique** Serious chip carvers use special knives, but quite reasonable results can be achieved with a skew chisel. A V-tool with a long point is also used for clearing waste wood from crevices.

The basic principle of chip carving is very much the same as that used for cutting notches in a stick with a penknife. Firstly a downward cut is made, followed by angled cuts on either side (Fig 11.22) to make intricate patterns. Fig 11.23 illustrates a typical traditional design, executed in simple form in Fig 11.24, which also shows examples of how chip-carving patterns can be used for decorating borders.

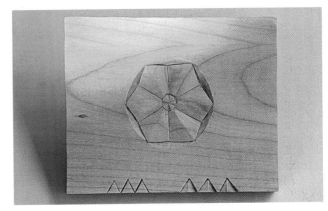

Fig 11.24 *A simple chip-carved flower, and simple V and diamond-V borders*

Summary

- Use the incised method for table and chair decorations, or whenever the surrounding surface needs to be kept flat, or when you simply need to 'draw' in the wood.

- Use the modified incised method for better light reflection.

- Use the intaglio style when the detail to be worked is too small or delicate for the wood to accept other carving methods, or when you want to produce a simple design quickly.

- Keep to simple designs for all three techniques, as they are much easier to work.

- Plan your cutting sequence before you start, as with all three methods you will have little chance of correcting mistakes.

- Try not to be over-ambitious, and avoid working to too great a depth.

- Work in sympathy with the wood, going with the lie of the grain for bright, clean cuts.

- Chip carving makes simple border patterns which can be used with effect on furniture.

- Make sure your tools are really sharp. All these styles suffer in appearance if they have been heavily sanded.

12 pierced carving

The essence of pierced work is to produce tracery with a sense or feeling of spatial lightness. It is impossible to achieve the same degree of effect with other forms of decorative carving.

This type of work used to be very popular. You will find beautiful examples of pierced carving in old churches, where the technique was used to fashion rood screens of considerable delicacy. Similarly, for centuries the pierced method has been widely used by Indian carvers for both temple and house decoration. It is a style which should not be overlooked by any aspiring woodcarver. The technique is not as difficult as it may first appear. Even a simple design will teach you about cutting wood delicately, and it can be tremendously satisfying.

Project: Wall plaque in pierced carving

The tracery panel described in this chapter serves to illustrate all the main points of pierced carving. This style is especially suitable for wall plaques, where the colour and texture of the wall itself will be visible through the negative areas. An attractive variation which you might like to try is to back the plaque with mirror glass.

Wood selection

You need to be very selective in the type of wood you use. It must be stable, well seasoned, and certainly close-grained: lime, sycamore, walnut or cherry are ideal. Unless you have a specific requirement, keep to a prepared thickness of about ¾in (20mm), as beyond this too much of the underside of the carving can become visible.

Design

Choose a fairly simple design for your first attempt. Lots of interlacing elements may look all very well on paper, but can be exasperating to carve. As with other types of carving, plan your design with some reference to the sizes of your tools.

Fig 12.1 *Starting to remove waste wood from a pierced carving; elements such as stems are left oversize to allow freedom in their final placing*

Much of the pierced effect is obtained from the shapes of the cut-out, or negative, parts of the design. When drawing, it is worthwhile shading or hatching these areas to see how they look. You could have both positive and negative leaf shapes, for example, which works well on bold patterns but can tend to give a confused impression if too repetitive.

At all times keep in mind the practicalities of cutting and shaping the wood. A successful pierced carving needs sufficient inbuilt strength, and there is little merit in making the design so delicate that the carving is

impossible to finish. Once you have the carbon imprint on the wood, make sure you are entirely happy with the design. Look at the thickness of interlocking parts which lie on the cross grain, and avoid making them too slender. Note how the stems used in the example are oversized, to give some freedom when deciding their final position and shape.

Outlining and removing negative spaces

Take the precaution of cutting around the whole design with a V-tool to create a safety net before starting to remove waste from each negative space (Fig 12.1). You can use a jigsaw or a coping saw to cut the voids (Figs 12.2 and 12.3). Drill pilot holes first, in the waste area near the V-tool line. Make sure you keep the drill at right angles to the wood to avoid straying into the design itself. Always secure the wood with G-clamps when using power tools.

Fig 12.2 *Removing waste with a coping saw*

Fig 12.3 *Removing waste with a jigsaw*

Once as much of the waste as possible has been sawn away, trim back to the outline with suitable gouges (Fig 12.4). Do not use excessive force, though, or there is a risk of splitting the wood at the back. It may be necessary to clean up some areas with a rasp. However you do it, the sides must be kept true and at right angles to the front face of the work.

Fig 12.4 *Trimming back to the outline with a gouge*

Check progress regularly from different viewpoints. If you are doubtful, leave a little extra wood in place so that final adjustments can be made later.

Fixing the main contours

This next stage is much the same as for any low- or high-relief carving. Plot the levels needed with coloured chalk, as described previously (see page 69). Avoid keeping all the design on the original surface level – the effect will be too flat. Instead, try and incorporate as much contour variation as you can. If the carving is to be double-sided (that is, viewed from both front and back), you will need to mark the contours on both sides. In the low areas, do not cut away more than about three quarters of the excess wood, since you still have work to do on the back of the carving.

Much of the cutting can usually be done with a skew chisel, and its slicing action will assist in cutting against the lie of the grain. When using a gouge (Fig 12.5), try to adopt the habit of using a slight twisting action, which reduces the pressure on the wood.

Fig 12.5 *Using a gouge to cut down to the low-lying areas; colour coding has been used to indicate the different levels*

Modelling

Then start to model roughly all the high-lying parts (Fig 12.6), keeping low parts in block form or they may become too weak. Use centre lines to help finalize the position of narrower elements (Fig 12.7).

Fig 12.6 *Roughly modelling high parts of the design with a gouge*

Fig 12.7 *Mark centre lines to establish the final position of narrow elements such as stems*

Undercutting

Once you have set in the design to approximately the depths you require, you can remove the surplus wood from the back (if your carving is single-sided). The extent of undercutting will depend on how you want the carving ultimately to be viewed. For example, if the carving is only to be seen from some distance you will not require a great degree of delicacy. But if viewed from just a few paces, more refined treatment will be called for. **Undercutting** means removing wood from the outer edges of the design at a fairly steep angle (see pages 83–4), and in pierced carving is known as **feather-edging**.

Shaping from the back

Some shaping from the back will be necessary, or there will be a disproportionate difference in thickness between the low and high areas. It is not necessary to think in true three-dimensional terms, as this could cause the carving to become structurally very weak. All that is ever needed is to feather-edge wider surfaces, such as leaves and petals, and to give the stems and branches a flat-bottomed oval sectional shape. A rasp or small riffler file will help in difficult areas (Fig 12.8); another useful tool is a rotary cutter fitted to a minidrill (Fig 12.9). Again, regularly check progress by standing the carving up and viewing it from different angles.

Generally, both undercutting and shaping from the back are carried out as one operation.

Completing the carving

Once you have cleared away the surplus wood from the rear, turn the carving over and finish modelling the front. After this you may find there is still some wood at the back requiring attention, but make sure you don't get carried away. At this stage you will not have much, if any, spare wood left to correct mistakes.

Fig 12.10 shows the completed carving. The natural colour of the wood seemed too light, so I changed it to a slightly darker shade, as described in the next chapter.

Before using the wood dye, the V-tool was used to add veins to the leaves. Also, fine texture cuts were made to the petals using the small no. 9 gouge. Light sanding was used to soften their outline so that they assumed a more natural look.

Fig 12.8 *Using a riffler file to feather-edge the back of a single-sided carving*

Fig 12.9 *A rotary cutter fitted to a miniature drill is also useful for feather-edging*

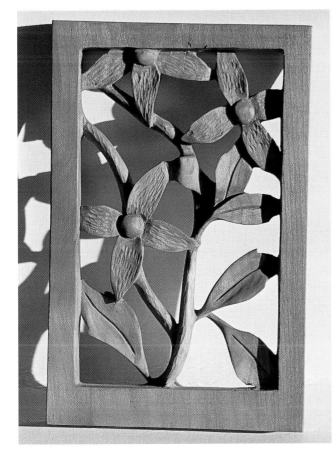

Fig 12.10 *The completed carving, showing fine texture cuts*

Summary

- Choose the design with some reference to the effect created by the negative voids. If you wish, relate spaces to positive elements.

- Make sure there is strength to the design, but aim to give the carving a feeling of lightness.

- Use stable, close-grained wood which is not too hard.

- Make sure you work in the waste wood outside the V-trench before cutting out negative parts.

- Avoid using too much force, as this could damage the structure. Carve with a light touch.

- Repeatedly check progress from different viewpoints.

13 colouring wood

Carvings are generally left showing the natural colour and figuring of the wood. Wetting the wood with water will give you an idea of its colour when polished. However, some timbers can appear too bland and uninteresting, and if the carving is to be applied to a piece of furniture there may be considerable mismatch of colour tone. For either of these reasons, you may want to colour the wood.

The colouring of wood is by no means a new idea. From earliest times ochres, earth pigments, herbs and other wild plants have been used as sources of colour. Much medieval carving was treated using these naturally produced dyes. Later, chemical dyes were developed to provide fade-free colours, and it was discovered that both oak and chestnut could be darkened by fuming with ammonia vapour.

Nowadays wood can be lightened, darkened or completely changed in colour with comparative ease, and the materials are readily available (Fig 13.1). Carvings can also be delicately tinted. Light-coloured woods such as wild cherry can be given a warm and pleasant look with 'antique pine' wood dye, as shown in Fig 13.2. More dramatic effects can be achieved by using stronger-toned dyes.

The use of colour in either minor or major modes can certainly enhance a piece of work; equally, if used with total abandon it can have a disastrous effect. Some preliminary thought should always be given to the effect you wish to achieve, and wherever possible tests should first be made on scrap wood or offcuts from the actual timber used. You may need to repeat part of the design on an offcut, just to test out the colour effect, but time spent doing this is worth it. Never colour a carving without first testing.

Sometimes you may wish to colour only part of a carving: you might want to darken the background while leaving the design area in the original colour; or perhaps the other way around. In these cases, treat the parts you want to leave in the natural colour with a heavy coating of wax (you do not need to buff it). This acts as a barrier, and prevents the dye penetrating these areas when you colour the rest of the carving.

● **Stain or dye?** Before looking in detail at some of the colour finishes you can use, it is worth clearing up a point which many people find confusing: what is the difference between a wood stain and a wood dye? In the old days, when life was simple, there never was any problem: father stained the bedroom floor while mother dyed her hair. It was as simple as that, and everyone knew what you meant if you said you were going to stain a piece of wood.

These days, however, the term **wood dye** is used to describe finishes suitable for use indoors, whereas **woodstain** – now one word – relates to an exterior grade of treatment. This is a point to note should you ever need to colour a carving kept outdoors. In this section we shall be looking at some of the treatments suitable for carvings kept indoors. To simplify matters I have used the Liberon range of products as examples.

Water-based dyes

These dyes are very traditional and some have been around for a very long time, such as vandyke crystals (made from walnut husks) or bichromate of potash. More recently, acrylic dyes have come to be generally used. They are available pre-mixed in a wide colour range and are very convenient to handle. Being water-based, the colour density can easily be changed.

Water-based dyes (Fig 13.3) are easy to use, and are applied with a sponge or brush. They are slow to penetrate, so any surplus can be dabbed off with a piece of plain paper kitchen towel to vary colour density at will.

With some 'fluffy' woods, like lime, you will find the grain can rise as the dye dries, necessitating some sanding back. This effect can be reduced if the wood is wetted with cold water and allowed to dry before applying the dye, so any raised grain can be removed at that

Fig 13.1 A selection of commercial wood dyes

Fig 13.2 *Giving a warmer tone to the pierced carving project from Chapter 12. A foam applicator is being used to apply the dye*

stage rather than after colouring. Be sure to sand gently, with the lie of the grain.

Spirit dyes

Spirit-based dyes penetrate deeply. They may be preferable if the wood has a high natural oil content or a substantial resin content, as both these properties tend to repel the water-based varieties. If you are in any doubt as to which type of dye to use, test both on a piece of scrap wood.

Spirit dyes react quickly when applied to bare wood, and their density can be difficult to control, especially when the end grain is porous. This can lead to a blotchy finish.

In order to obtain a more uniform finish, some pre-sealing of end grain may be necessary. Do this with the application of some white spirit (mineral spirit) before using the dye. Sometimes a weaker solution of the dye may be used to stain end grain. It is best to use a pad of cloth and to apply the dye in small quantities, as application by brush is more difficult to control.

Concentrated dyes

Concentrated dyes are available in both spirit-based and water-based forms, and can be added to standard dyes to alter or strengthen the colour.

Translucent finishes

These finishes let the wood grain show through the colour. In some instances this can be an advantage, but translucent finishes seldom give you a complete colour change. As an alternative to proprietary makes you can use artists' waterproof drawing inks.

Other colouring methods

It is possible to colour wood with vegetable dyes, such as the culinary types which come in little bottles – or you could even try boiling up handfuls of leaves or roots yourself. The results may not be very satisfactory, though, and rarely justify the time and effort involved. It is generally far better to buy reputable products specially designed for the purpose.

Fig 13.3 *Using a selection of Liberon's Palette series dyes to colour a simple flower design*

If you need only a very small amount of colour, use watered-down artists' acrylic paints. Experiment with colour density and dilution on a piece of scrap wood.

How many colours do you need?

There are two approaches to this question. Most dye manufacturers offer a wide range of pre-mixed colours (Liberon's Palette series, for example, has 22 colours), which can be intermixed at will or added to with concentrated dyes to give a vast total range. Alternatively, you can work with the primary colours: red, blue and yellow. By mixing combinations of these, adding black or white to darken or lighten, an approximation of all other colours can be achieved.

When and how to use dyes

The degree of colour is very personal. A simple example would be when the undercut parts of relief carvings are darkened to increase the shadow contrast. Much old furniture carving was subjected to this treatment, but the choice of whether or not to use the technique is entirely up to you. Complex colouring can completely change the look of a carving.

Incised carving can be 'strengthened' if the cut lines are darkened (Fig 13.4). Before carving, the wood should be sealed with sanding sealer or a diluted matt varnish.

You may want only a subtle colour change to give a warm look to bland wood, as mentioned earlier, or perhaps a dramatic polychromatic effect is needed. Refer back to the final photograph of the low-relief flower carving in Chapter 8 (page 85), which shows the untreated limewood. Compare this with Fig 13.3, which shows a very similar carving in the process of being coloured with water dyes from the Palette range.

To give the work luminosity, gilt powder can be sprinkled on and rubbed in once the dyes are dry. A spray fixative can then be used, and the carving can finally be sealed with matt acrylic varnish.

Fig 13.4 *An example of an incised pattern enhanced by darkening the line*

Gilt effects

It isn't difficult to obtain a gilded effect, and you don't have to go to the expense of using gold leaf. In all cases, though, gilding is more effective when the wood has been crisply carved.

First seal the wood with Fontenay base priming coat (available from Liberon and from some antique restorers) and allow it to dry thoroughly (Fig 13.5). The base comes in different colours for different finishes: red for antique gold; yellow for bright gilt; black for silver or pewter effects.

Apply gilt varnish carefully with a paintbrush (Fig 13.6). There are eight traditional shades, ranging from bright gilt to old gold and shades of silver and bronze. Always test your choice on scrap wood before you work on your carving.

An aged look can be produced by rubbing back the gilt varnish when dry, to let the base coat show through. This needs to be done with restraint, and it is usually confined to parts of the carving that could have worn over the passage of time, such as high spots, edges or corners.

Fuming

This is an old practice using ammonia, which only works with woods containing tannic acid, such as oak and chestnut. It produces a warm colour, the degree of which depends on the length of time the wood is exposed to the ammonia vapour. Being the result of a chemical reaction, the look of fumed wood is quite different from the effect of using a dye.

All you need to fume wood is a reasonably airtight container to take the carving or furniture. You can make up a polythene tent, or use a garden cloche or dustbin. I even used the inside of a truck once for a very large table. You can use normal household ammonia cleaner, bought at a hardware store (Fig 13.7), and usually need only a shallow dish to hold the ammonia. If you are going

Fig 13.5 *Applying Fontenay base*

Fig 13.6 *Using gilt varnish*

to fume a large piece of work, or if there is a large volume of air in your container, you will need to double up on the number of dishes. Put the ammonia in the airtight container with the carving. After about two, or possibly three, hours of exposure to the ammonia vapour the wood will have turned to a mid-tone. The longer the wood is exposed to the ammonia fumes, the darker it will get. (For an example, see page 111.)

After fuming, wash the wood with cold water and leave it to dry naturally before coating it with finishing oil and/or wax. Do take every precaution when using ammonia, and avoid touching it or breathing the fumes. It can be harmful to your eyes, so be sure to wear goggles.

Fig 13.7 *Use household ammonia to fume oak or chestnut*

Summary

- The most important thing is to experiment with colour.

- Use the same species of wood to make tests.

- If you want to colour only part of a carving, seal and wax the remainder before using any dye.

- Water dyes work slowly, and are very easy to use.

- Spirit dyes react fast, and soak into end grain quickly. They can cause a blotchy look, so seal absorbent areas with diluted matt polyurethane varnish.

14 a gallery of carvings

Chair back

Mahogany

Believed to have been carved c.1860 by Theophilus Williams,
the author's great-grandfather

Spinning stool

Oak

Designed and carved by Jeremy Williams;
stool made by David White
(Photographs: David Scholes)

Floral swag

Lime, 30 x 7½ x 3in (760 x 185 x 75mm)

Designed and carved by David C. Bevan

Four salvers

Designed and carved by Peter Boex

All 16in (405mm) diameter

(Photographs: Peter Boex)

Daffodil salver

Chestnut

Foxglove salver

Chestnut

Vine leaf salver

Oak

Daffodil salver

Sycamore

appendix: technical drawing

While much relief carving involves free-form drawing, there are times when it is necessary to use a more formal approach, often based on geometric principles. The following may be found useful in formulating designs.

For accuracy of working, good-quality drawing instruments are recommended. Use a screw-adjustable compass, or one which can be locked to a setting. For plotting directly on to wood, however, pointed dividers are usually more accurate.

Basic constructions

To bisect a line (Fig A.1)

Open the compass to more than half the length of the line **AB**. With point on **A**, and then on **B**, strike arcs above and below the line. Then join the intersections of these arcs above and below the line.

The line you have constructed divides **AB** into two equal parts and is at right angles to it.

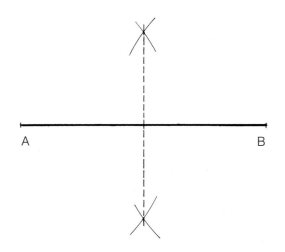

Fig A.1 *Bisecting a line*

To bisect an angle (Fig A.2)

Angle **XYZ**. Place compass point on **Y** and strike an arc to cut **XY** and then **ZY**.

With compass at same setting, place point at arc on **XY** and strike an arc between the two arms of the angle. Do the same from the point on **ZY**.

Where these new arcs intersect, draw a line to point **Y**. This line will bisect the angle.

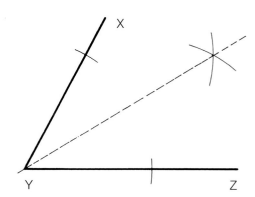

Fig A.2 *Bisecting an angle*

To construct a well-proportioned rectangle, creating a golden section (Fig A.3)

First draw a square. Bisect the bottom line to find the midpoint **A**.

Place your compass point on **A** and open the compass to the top right corner of the square **B**. Then scribe an arc to meet the extended base line at **C**.

Complete the rectangle.

The rectangle can be divided into a square, and a rectangle which is proportionally identical to the original rectangle. The new rectangle can be further subdivided in the same proportion to help fix points of design interest.

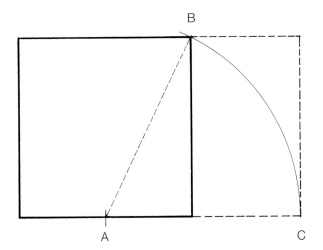

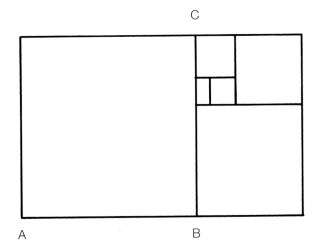

Fig A.3 *Creating a golden rectangle*

Fig A.4 *Subdividing a golden rectangle into squares and equally proportioned smaller rectangles*

To form a square and rectangle inside the golden rectangle (Fig A.4)

Set compass to short side of rectangle from point **A**. Swing arc to cut long side of rectangle at **B** and draw perpendicular to **C**.

Repeat as desired for each smaller rectangle.

To construct a regular polygon having equal sides (Fig A.5)

A polygon is a shape with any number of sides greater than four.

First draw a circle approximately the size of the polygon you require.

Then draw the vertical diameter **BC**.

Divide **BC** into the same number of equal parts as there are sides of the polygon.

In the diagram the diameter has been divided into five equal parts by drawing line **BD** from point **B** at an angle, and of a length easily divided into five equal parts by measurement. Point **D** is joined to **5** on line **BC**. Other lines are then drawn parallel to it to divide the diameter at the other four points.

Then with compass point on **C** and opened to **B** strike an arc on the horizontal diameter extended out to **A**.

With compass point on **B**, strike a second arc to intersect the first arc at **A**.

Join point **A** to point **2** and extend to cut the circumference at **E**.

BE is one side of the polygon. Step round the circle with compass set to the distance **BE** to complete the polygon.

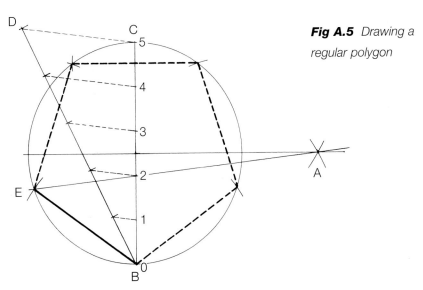

Fig A.5 *Drawing a regular polygon*

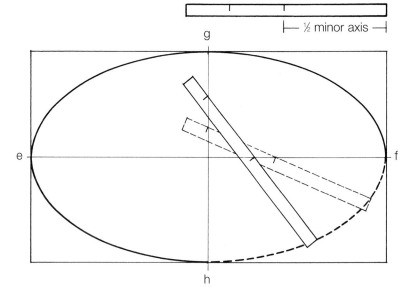

Fig A.6 Drawing an ellipse

To draw an ellipse (Fig A.6)

The size of your panel may determine the length and width of the ellipse you require.

The length **ef** is the **major axis** and the width **gh** the **minor axis**. Draw these two lines on your rectangle.

Make a trammel from a strip of card. Mark on it half the major axis and half the minor axis.

Place the trammel on the axis lines, so that the point marked for half major axis always touches the minor axis, and the point marked for half minor axis always touches the major axis.

As you slide the trammel to sweep each quarter, mark points at the trammel end. After you have finished marking all the points, then join them up with a fair curve to form the ellipse.

Tracery panels

Tracery panels often necessitate drawing circles inside other geometric shapes. The following constructions are useful for this.

Circles within squares (Figs A.7–A.9)

Diagonals are used to determine centres (Figs A.7 and A.8). In the final square, Fig A.9, the angle at **A** has been bisected to cut the centre line in order to find the centre of the first circle.

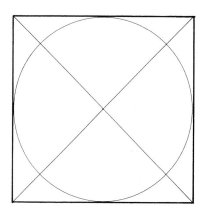

Fig A.7 Drawing a circle within a square

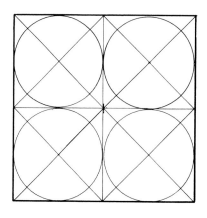

Fig A.8 Drawing circles within a square

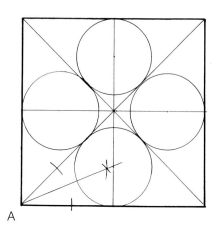

Fig A.9 Circles within a square

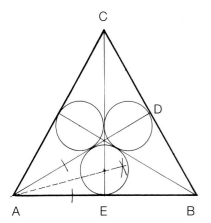

Fig A.10 *Drawing circles within a triangle*

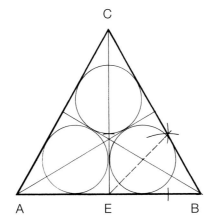

Fig A.11 *Circles within a triangle*

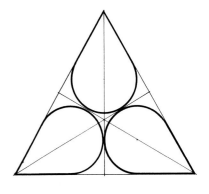

Fig A.12 *Extending the circles to form a trefoil-type design*

Circles within triangles (Figs A.10–A.12)

Start by using the construction shown in Fig A.1 to bisect each side of the triangle. Angle **DAB** is bisected, and the point where it intersects the line **EC** gives the centre for the first circle. Use this radius to form the other two circles.

In Fig A.11, angle **CEB** is bisected to intersect the line drawn to bisect the angle **ABC**.

Use the distance from **B** to the centre of the circle to find the centres of the remaining two circles.

This construction can be developed into the final trefoil-type design (Fig A.12).

Circles within polygons (Figs A.13 and A.14)

The polygon is divided into triangles, and then the previous constructions can be used.

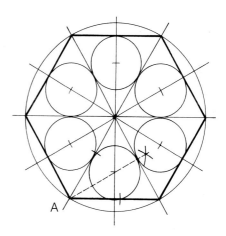

Fig A.13 *Drawing circles within polygons*

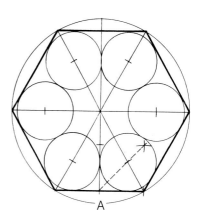

Fig A.14 *Circles within polygons*

Petal tracery (Fig A.15)

For petal tracery you need to set out a double hexagon (a 12-sided figure).

Keeping the compass set at the radius used to draw your basic circle, step round the circumference to find the first hexagon (6-sided figure).

Join one side of the hexagon **AB**. Bisect **AB** to find the midpoint, which will cut the circumference at a point **X** on the second hexagon.

Use the compass set at the same radius to step round the circle from **X**, marking the remaining 5 points of the second hexagon.

Place the compass point at each of the 12 points and scribe a semicircle, using the radius of the basic circle.

Archimedean spiral

Drawing a scroll using an Archimedean spiral (Fig A.16)

Decide the starting and finishing points of your spiral. These are marked **A** and **B** on the radius of the circle, centre **P**. **AB** is then divided into 12 equal parts.

The circle is divided into 12 equal segments (see Fig A.15 for 12-sided figures).

Draw an arc joining point **1** on radius **BP** to radius **no. 1**.

Take each point thereafter on radius **BP**, in sequence, and describe arcs to intersect their appropriate radii.

Draw a fair curve through these points to form the Archimedean spiral.

Fig A.15 *Drawing a 12-petalled flower*

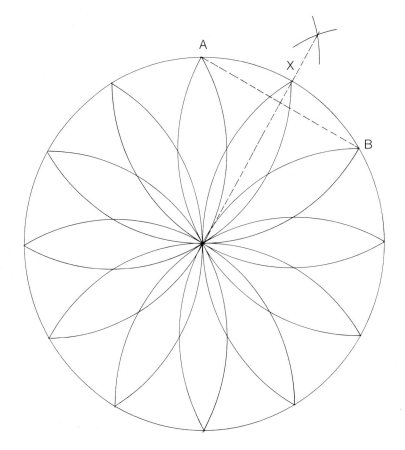

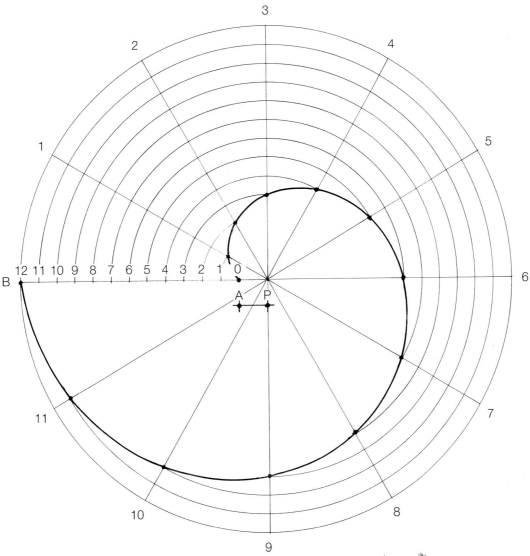

Fig A.16 *Drawing a scroll using an Archimedean spiral*

Ionic volute

Drawing an Ionic volute (Fig A.17)

A scroll can be drawn using a whelk or similar spiral shell. A large coach screw can also be used.

Tie cotton to the point of a pencil, then wind the cotton round the shell, following the spiral, so that the pencil point finishes close to the small, pointed end of the shell.

Unwind the cotton while holding the shell still; this permits the pencil to draw an Ionic volute.

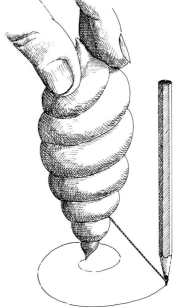

Fig A.17 *Using a shell to draw an Ionic volute*

imperial/metric conversion table

measurements

Although care has been taken to ensure that metric measurements in the text are true and accurate, they are only conversions from imperial; they have been rounded up or down to the nearest whole millimetre, or to the nearest convenient equivalent in cases where the imperial measurements themselves are only approximate. When following the projects, use either the metric or the imperial measurements; do not mix units.

inches to millimetres

inches	mm	inches	mm	inches	mm
⅛	3	9	229	30	762
¼	6	10	254	31	787
⅜	10	11	279	32	813
½	13	12	305	33	838
⅝	16	13	330	34	864
¾	19	14	356	35	889
⅞	22	15	381	36	914
1	25	16	406	37	940
1¼	32	17	432	38	965
1½	38	18	457	39	991
1¾	44	19	483	40	1016
2	51	20	508	41	1041
2½	64	21	533	42	1067
3	76	22	559	43	1092
3½	89	23	584	44	1118
4	102	24	610	45	1143
4½	114	25	635	46	1168
5	127	26	660	47	1194
6	152	27	686	48	1219
7	178	28	711	49	1245
8	203	29	737	50	1270

about the author

Jeremy Williams started carving at the age of 14. His family's connection with woodcarving can be traced back to the early part of the nineteenth century. He has practised professionally, with work sold widely both in England and overseas.

Jeremy is a fully qualified instructor with extensive teaching experience in Adult Education Centres, including Salisbury College of Technology, and Cornwall College.

For many years he ran private courses from his studio in the south-west of England. Nowadays he devotes his time to writing about woodcarving, with regular contributions to *Woodcarving* magazine.

Jeremy is the author of three books on carving.

index

Gardening

Alpine Gardening
Auriculas for Everyone: How to Grow and Sh
  Perfect Plants
Beginners' Guide to Herb Gardening
Beginners' Guide to Water Gardening
Bird Boxes and Feeders for the Garden
The Birdwatcher's Garden
Broad-Leaved Evergreens
Companions to Clematis: Growing Clematis
  with Other Plants
Creating Contrast with Dark Plants
Creating Small Habitats for Wildlife in your C
Exotics are Easy
Gardening with Hebes
Gardening with Wild Plants
Growing Cacti and Other Succulents in the
  Conservatory and Indoors
Growing Cacti and Other Succulents
  in the Garden
Hardy Palms and Palm-Like Plants
Hardy Perennials: A Beginner's Guide
Hedges: Creating Screens and Edges
The Living Tropical Greenhouse: Creating a
  Haven for Butterflies
Marginal Plants
Orchids are Easy: A Beginner's Guide to
  their Care and Cultivation
Plant Alert: A Garden Guide for Parents
Planting Plans for Your Garden
Plants that Span the Seasons
Sink and Container Gardening Using Dwa
  Hardy Plants
The Successful Conservatory and Growing
  Exotic Plants
Success with Orchids in the Greenhouse
  and Conservatory
Tropical Garden Style with Hardy Plants
Water Garden Projects: From Groundwork
  to Planting

Photography

Close-Up on Insects
Double Vision
An Essential Guide to Bird Photography
Field Guide to Bird Photography
Field Guide to Landscape Photography
How to Photograph Pets
In my Mind's Eye: Seeing in Black and White
Life in the Wild: A Photographer's Year
Light in the Landscape: A Photographer's Year
Outdoor Photography Portfolio
Photographing Fungi in the Field
Photography for the Naturalist
Viewpoints from Outdoor Photography
Where and How to Photograph Wildlife

Art Techniques

Garden: A Guide for Beginners Rachel Shirley

David James
David James
David Springett
David Springett
Dennis White
Dennis White
Dennis White
Dennis White
Dennis White
Dennis White
Jim Kingshott
Jim Kingshott
John Jordan
John Jordan
Keith Rowley
Ray Gonzalez
Alan Goodsell
John Burke

...dcarving
...tmaking
...oodworking
...lagazine
...raphy
...aphy
...tography
... News
...ers

Steve Young
Steve Young
Peter Watson
Nick Ridley
Charlie Waite
Andy Rouse
Peter Watson
GMC Publications
George McCarthy
Mark Lucock
GMC Publications
Peter Evans

...tles currently published
...ublished.
...Publishers or through
...specialist retailers.

To place an order, or to obtain a complete catalogue,
contact:

GMC Publications,
Castle Place, 166 High Street, Lewes,
East Sussex BN7 1XU, United Kingdom
Tel: 01273 488005 Fax: 01273 478606
E-mail: pubs@thegmcgroup.com

Orders by credit card are accepted